Planning and Budgeting Skills for Health and Social Work Managers

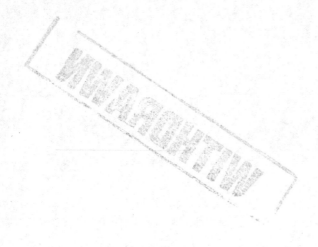

Planning and Budgeting Skills for Health and Social Work Managers

RICHARD FIELD

Series Editor: Keith Brown

Los Angeles | London | New Delhi
Singapore | Washington DC

www.learningmatters.co.uk

Los Angeles | London | New Delhi
Singapore | Washington DC

Learning Matters
An imprint of SAGE Publications Ltd
1 Oliver's Yard
55 City Road
London EC1Y 1SP

SAGE Publications Inc.
2455 Teller Road
Thousand Oaks, California 91320

SAGE Publications India Pvt Ltd
B 1/I 1 Mohan Cooperative Industrial Area
Mathura Road
New Delhi 110 044

SAGE Publications Asia-Pacific Pte Ltd
3 Church Street
#10-04 Samsung Hub
Singapore 049483

Editor: Luke Block
Development editor: Lauren Simpson
Production controller: Chris Marke
Project management: Swales & Willis Ltd, Exeter,
Devon
Marketing manager: Tamara Navaratnam
Cover design: Wendy Scott
Typeset by: Swales & Willis Ltd, Exeter, Devon
Printed by: TJ International Ltd, Padstow, Cornwall

Library of Congress Control Number: 2011945611

British Library Cataloguing in Publication Data

A catalogue record for this book is available from
the British Library

ISBN 978 1 44625 672 5
ISBN 978 0 85725 987 5 (pbk)

Contents

List of figures

List of tables

List of activities

Foreword

Many professionals in health and social care find one day that they have a new role: one of being a manager, and with this comes the responsibility for planning and budgeting within their organisations. Prior to this their training and development has been in a specific professional field in order to develop specific professional skills, knowledge and competence.

If you are one of these managers who has clear professional skills but has never formally engaged in leadership and management development then this text is for you. It is expertly written so that planning and budgeting skills are understandable and accessible. The text gives clear guidelines and tips on how to plan and budget effectively within a health and social care context and this is due in large part to Richard Field's expert knowledge as an accountant, academic and leadership consultant within the field of health and social care.

This text is one of a new series designed to support frontline social work/care leadership and management development. The series is designed to meet the learning needs and capabilities as set out in the 'Leadership and Management Development for Social Work and Social Care: Creating Leadership Pathways of Progression' strategy by Jane Holroyd, MBE and Professor Keith Brown (2011).

I commend this text to you and trust it will help you achieve the best possible health and social care in our society.

Keith Brown
Series Editor
Director of Centre for Post Qualifying Social Work, Bournemouth University

About the author

Richard Field is a qualified accountant and management development specialist who has extensive experience of working with managers and leaders across the public, voluntary and private sectors.

Having worked in local government as an accountant and in the university sector as a principal lecturer Richard became a freelance management development specialist in 1992. During the last twenty years Richard has helped hundreds of social care managers develop competence in planning and budgeting and advised many public and voluntary organisations on the development of effective approaches to planning and budgeting.

Acknowledgements

The author would like to thank all those managers who have shared their stories about how planning and budget management actually occurs within their organisations.

Section 1
Introduction

This text is written primarily as a practitioner guide for managers engaged in planning and budgeting within health and social care organisations. The aim is to promote effective approaches to planning and budget management within organisations and prompt the development of associated competence.

Two main health and social care audiences are envisaged:

- students undertaking academic programmes that feature planning and budgeting; and
- managers wishing to refresh, challenge and extend their practice.

In addition, this text will also be of assistance to managers in other parts of the public and voluntary sector.

This text focuses on:

- plans that are used for managerial rather than professional or personal purposes;
- planning processes and tools that can be used in many managerial situations; and
- budget preparation and control as practiced by managers rather than accountants.

The planning content is concerned primarily with business level strategy within an organisation rather than corporate or operational strategy. Johnson *et al.* (2008: 596) describe business level strategy as being 'about how to compete successfully in particular markets' – recognising that for public service organisations the equivalent concern is how to provide 'best value' (p224). Likewise, content relating to budget management is primarily aimed at cost centres rather than corporate management.

For planning and budgeting to be included in the same book is quite unusual as professionally, organisationally and academically these two processes are often separated. However, there is a growing recognition of the need for planning and budgeting to be integrated, the case for which is made later. For now it is sufficient to say that where integration occurs managers will find it easier to engage in both processes and are likely to be more effective.

This book presents planning and budgeting in the order in which these should occur within organisations; that is planning first, from which budgeting should flow.

This book includes:

- written material intended to develop basic understanding of planning and budget management;
- activities designed to cause engagement with organisational practices related to planning and budget management; and
- tips for success considered central to 'cracking' effective planning and budget management.

Section 2
Planning – an introduction

This section introduces planning from personal and organisational perspectives, identifies common variations in planning practice and explains how these are influenced by personality and context.

What is planning?

Planning can be defined as the process by which a desired future state is conceived and an effective way of delivering this developed and resourced.

This statement makes three important points:

- planning concerns design, which should be a creative and, hopefully, enjoyable process;
- planning is future based and should be aspirational, involving thinking beyond the current situation and any actual or perceived limitations;
- planning involves identifying a way of making a desired future a reality.

Personal aspects of planning

All people plan. To completely avoid planning would require a person to act in an entirely spontaneous way, never thinking about what they might do next. Arguably, even a decision *not* to plan is actually a form of planning – it is a decision about what to do or how to behave in the future.

During their life, an individual working within health and social care may engage in a variety of planning, for example:

- personal planning (e.g. career, lifestyle, pensions);
- care or treatment planning (e.g. care package and patient treatment);
- workload planning with regard to what they intend to do today, this month or this year;
- team planning with colleagues;
- planning for an establishment such as a doctors' practice or day centre;
- planning for a service such as chiropody or home care;
- planning for a major part of an organisation (e.g. a department, directorate or speciality);
- planning for an organisation (e.g. a voluntary organisation or hospital);
- planning with other agencies to commission or provide a service (e.g. youth offending);
- planning in respect of a project.

While we all plan, the extent to which we do so, and our approach, are influenced by personality and context. As individuals we differ in terms of:

- the pleasure we derive from planning;
- the time we are prepared to devote to planning;
- how early or late we start to plan;
- the level of detail we include in our plans;
- the extent to which we engage others in planning;
- how easy we find it to depart from or change plans.

Comparing how two people prepare for a holiday illustrates this natural variation:

EXAMPLE

Person A starts planning their holiday six months ahead, booking flights and hotels, organising activities and making lists of what needs to be taken, using a spreadsheet to estimate and track costs. This person packs during the week before they go, ticking items off their list and double-checking their itinerary and timings before they fly.

Person B books their flights and hotel four weeks before their intended departure date, finds out what sort of activities are available but leaves booking these until they get to their destination. Packing is done the day before departure without a list and in the belief that anything forgotten can be purchased on arrival.

Both holidaymakers engage in planning. While the second person starts later and engages in less detail, planning has nonetheless occurred. Person B might actually prefer to 'take off' when they like but in practice will complete one or two actions in advance, perhaps because they:

- have young children that they do not wish to take out of school;
- wish to ensure their children are safe and secure and recognise that less planned or spontaneous holidays might involve 'roughing it';
- are in employment and need organisational approval for absence;
- do not wish to let colleagues down by disappearing at short notice.

How the two holidaymakers actually behave is likely to reflect their natural preferences as modified to fit the context.

One common difference between personal and organisational planning is that few of us in our private lives will prepare written plans. More usually, the product of our planning is held in our memory, captured on a calendar, or as a list of jobs to do, etc. Taking domestic decorating as an example – even those people who enjoy planning, and know which rooms they intend to decorate next, are unlikely to prepare a written three-year 'home decoration and renewal plan'.

Organisational aspects of planning

As with individuals, the amount of planning within an organisation and the way this is undertaken varies. All organisations engage in planning to some extent and in most instances this results in a plan document. In the private sector, a significant driver for preparing plans is the need to secure loans and overdraft facilities. Similarly, voluntary organisations require bank support but also need to influence or satisfy the interests of potential funders, so again are likely to prepare plans. Statutory sector organisations are likely to prepare plans because of a need to satisfy the requirements or expectations of the government and other agencies. In the current environment it is, therefore, virtually impossible to avoid preparing organisational plans.

Although the format of a plan may be externally imposed, there is normally freedom about the process by which this is prepared and the priority and resources given in support; this tending to reflect the personal preferences of powerful stakeholders.

Where organisational planning is less valued, the plan document may fulfil the requirements of external stakeholders but only limited use will be made of this within the organisation. Often, there is a sense of 'going through the motions' with plan content based largely on what has happened before rather than on a considered analysis of what should happen in future. Documents prepared this way tend to lack vision, are operational in nature and lack linkage to the budget – a combination that leaves service managers vulnerable to 'across the board' budget cuts as they are unable to explain the value of what they plan to do or how this links with the resources they claim to need. Mintzberg (1994: 156) makes the case for strategic thinking, the outcome of which should be 'an integrated perspective of the enterprise, a not too precisely articulated vision of direction'. Integration involves bringing together insights about many aspects of the service or organisation, including the external environment within which the organisation will operate. This thinking, combined with a degree of creativity, helps those planning to challenge existing practice and assumption.

Organisations that are led by planning enthusiasts are more likely to have a sound planning process and prepare plan documents that go beyond what is required by external agencies.

Planning can make a significant contribution to effective management particularly when integrated with performance management, budgeting and other processes; these collectively ensure that planned activity is resourced, progress is monitored and prompt control action is taken.

Planning context

Since coming to power in May 2010 the Conservative/Liberal Democrat coalition has set about reform at a fast pace, sweeping away institutions, reducing centrally driven performance measures, launching the 'big society', pursuing localism and acting to reduce the country's financial deficit. These actions combine to significantly affect the context within which public services will be expected to perform, the type of plans that will be required in future and the skills needed to deliver the intended outcomes.

- Locality planning is likely to increase as communities exercise their 'right to challenge' and develop responses to prioritised needs and the expressed preferences of citizens.
- More planning will be undertaken on a multi-agency or community basis.
- State-funded service provision will increasingly be undertaken by private and third sector organisations operating along more commercial lines – the use of business plans and business cases is likely to increase.
- GPs who will be responsible for commissioning inpatient care from 2013 are likely to be more engaged in helping plan and deliver local responses to local issues.
- The 'right to provide' given to front line public sector employees and the growing tendency for public sector organisations to commission rather than provide will result in the establishment of a considerable number of social enterprises in the next few years, each requiring a robust business case and business plan.

- For an increasing number of organisations, survival will depend on winning business rather than simply waiting for a budget to be announced.
- Competition is likely to increase with more providers entering the market, a proportion of which will seek to trade across geographic areas.
- Commercial skills will become increasingly important.

Plans and budgets

Planning and budgeting should naturally link as shown in Figure 2.1, which assumes a three-year planning period. The plan incorporates a clear statement of purpose, measurable objectives and the key actions needed to achieve these. All activity, whether ongoing or new, requires physical resources such as staff time, buildings, equipment, medical supplies, etc. Plans should include a summary of the resources needed expressed in terms of quantity and quality which can then be converted into a financial budget by multiplying the quantity of each resource required by the appropriate price.

Once the plan, which includes the budget, has been prepared it should be subject to scrutiny to ensure it is challenging yet achievable. Mark Moore (1995: 28), professor at Harvard University's Kennedy School of Government, considers that the 'aim of managerial work in the public sector is to create public value, just as the aim of managerial work in the private sector is to create private value'. Increasingly higher performance from public service commissioners and providers is being demanded, the scope for which depends on a range of factors, including existing performance levels, changes in the operating environment, need, understanding what works and technological advances. The planning process offers a framework and an opportunity to pursue performance improvement.

Scrutiny should result in both the plan and budget being approved or rejected. As the budget is the financial expression of the money needed to acquire the physical resources required to deliver the plan, accepting the plan and rejecting the budget or vice versa is both illogical and unacceptable. Where the plan and budget are rejected, which is quite common, those planning have three main options:

1. change the objectives which will ultimately affect the volume and, or type of resources required;
2. change the actions by which objectives are intended to be achieved, thus affecting the type, mix and/or volume of resources required and, therefore, the budget;
3. change the physical resources that it is planned to use, for example skill mix, location etc.

Underpinning integration is a belief that if the planning and budgeting process is rigorous it will prove impossible to cut budgets without planned activity being affected in some way. It follows then that if organisational leaders wish to spend less money on a service they should recognise and take responsibility for the associated consequences which might involve lower service quantity, or reduced quality, ultimately leading to poorer outcomes.

If plans and budgets are linked, the manager will start the year with sufficient money to achieve the plan. If circumstances during the year differ from what was expected, resource consumption may be affected and managerial control action necessary.

While the above approach is logical, plans and budgets in this sector are rarely fully integrated, especially at lower organisational levels. Over time senior managers, politicians and the public in general have become accustomed to demanding greater service quantity and quality while expecting budgets to remain static, if not reduced year on year. Sadly, the practice of

Figure 2.1 Integrating plans and budgets

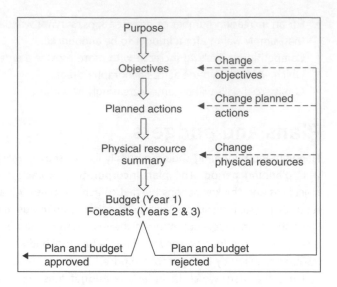

applying budget cuts across the board is still popular with key stakeholders who appear reluctant to make or be associated with unpopular service decisions.

TIPS FOR SUCCESS

- *Invest time and energy in understanding how much physical resource is needed to support your plan and be prepared to explain how this is calculated.*
- *At all times link your budget to your plan and resist changes made to one but not the other. This applies to plan/budget approval, when considering variations during the year, and to year-end performance reviews.*
- *Use the planning process as an opportunity for performance improvement.*
- *Remember – unless physical resources can be purchased more cheaply and/or worked harder it is impossible to cut an integrated budget without affecting intended outcomes.*

Why plan?

If planning is undertaken with care and enthusiasm it should:

- stimulate service development by challenging thinking and current practice;
- ensure that services and activities continue to be relevant;
- lead to sustainable performance improvement;
- increase individual and collective knowledge of the environment, service users and service operation;
- provide an early warning of possible opportunities and threats and offer decision makers greater choice regarding the pace of any changes they deem necessary;
- improve risk management;
- build future capacity in respect of leaders, managers, professional and other staff;
- lead to a shared sense of direction and a framework for decision making;
- provide a basis for performance management;

- provide an opportunity to engage service users, staff and partner agencies;
- provide a sense of purpose and direction for staff, thereby improving morale;
- assist other managerial processes, for example, budget management, facilities investment, staff development, etc.;
- provide evidence of the service being 'fit for business' which is important to funders and other stakeholders.

The above benefits are impressive but will only materialise if the planning process is effective and well resourced.

Types of plan

All organisations prepare plans, and these vary in format, length and title. The following list includes just a few of the plans currently found in the health and social care sector:

- care plan;
- strategic direction plan;
- business plan;
- joint investment plan;
- service plan;
- performance improvement plan;
- school development plan;
- local area plan;
- operational plan;
- strategic plan;
- corporate plan;
- youth justice plan.

In the public sector, different approaches to planning have been tried over the years, one notable example being business planning which emerged during the 1980s. Well known in the private sector, business planning proved to be rather alien to voluntary and public sector managers. Part of a wider movement to adopt a business paradigm, business planning was initially considered relevant to those parts of the public and voluntary sector that operate, or could operate, on business lines. In the 1980s and 1990s the use of business planning was seen in NHS Trusts, services covered by compulsory competitive tendering and by some in-house social care providers in local authorities and charities. In practice, business planning proved difficult to adopt as:

- it required a significant shift in thinking by managers and politicians;
- some terminology and many of the associated techniques need adjusting for successful use in a public service context; and
- the underpinning values can feel inappropriate in a health and social care context.

Over the next few years, policies pursued by the coalition government will cause many public sector employees to migrate to private sector providers or form arm's length organisations and social enterprises, all of which are likely to operate on business lines and engage in business planning.

Table 2.1 compares the typical, but not universal, characteristics of traditional service and business units. Plans can be categorised in a number of ways, including those in Table 2.2.

Table 2.1 Comparing service and business operations

Factor	Service operation	Business operation
Form of planning	Service planning	Business planning
Budgets	Few (mainly controllable) expenditure budgets	Expenditure and income budgets
Financial performance	Line by line, possibly bottom line net budget	Surplus/deficit or return
Identity	Less distinct	Branded
Planning level	Operational	Strategic/operational
Financial freedom	Comparatively low	Comparatively high
View of service recipients	Service users	Customers
See other providers as . . .	Alternative providers	Competitors

Table 2.2 Plan characteristics

Time frame	The period of time a plan relates to, e.g. short term (typically one year), medium term (typically three to five years) and long term (normally in excess of five years).
Compulsory and optional	A number of plans are prepared to meet the requirements of external agencies or to demonstrate best practice. Other plans are prepared because politicians, board members or senior managers consider these to be of potential value.
Scope	Plans may be prepared at different organisational levels relating to a unit, a service or the whole organisation. Often a hierarchy of plans can be found within an organisation.
Developmental or whole activity	Some plans focus only on those aspects of a service that need to be different in future and are developmental in nature. Other plans are whole in the sense that they address ongoing operation as well as new developments.
Fixed or rolling	Some plans are prepared for a fixed period of time at the end of which either the activity will cease or a new plan will be prepared. Other plans 'roll on'; each year a new plan is prepared for the full planning period. Taking a three-year rolling plan as an example, approval is specifically given for the first year's service activity and budget and outline approval is given for years two and three. During the latter part of year one a new three-year plan will be developed and specific approval will again be sought for the first year this contains, which might or might not differ from the outline detail included as year two in the current plan.
Strategic and operational	Strategic plans tend to be informed by analysis and critical thinking regarding the purpose, objectives and actions needed for long term success. By contrast operational plans are concerned with the detail of how activities are going to be managed this year.

ACTIVITY 2.1

Plan characteristics

This activity is intended to develop your understanding of planning in your organisation.

Identify the plan that is used to manage your service area and answer the following questions:

- *What time frame does it cover?*
- *Is the preparation of this plan compulsory?*
- *If the plan is compulsory, which agency requires its preparation?*
- *What is the scope of this document?*
- *Is it developmental or a whole service plan?*
- *Is it fixed or rolling?*
- *Is it strategic, operational or both?*

Plan format

One of the key issues to address when planning is the format to be used. For some managers there will be little choice as this is determined by external agencies or organisational leaders. Where this is not the case, either an existing plan format can be adopted or one can be designed for the specific context.

The format adopted in this book is based on three main sections – analysis, direction and action planning – depicted in Figure 2.2 as three triangles which combine to present planning proposals in a coherent and persuasive way.

The purpose and content of each section is as follows:

Analysis

The analysis section should help the reader to develop a good understanding of the current and likely future context for the plan. The content should include a mixture of historic, current and forecast information regarding various aspects of the service, for example, changes in the

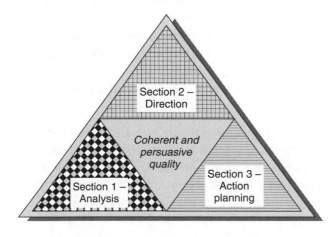

Figure 2.2 Plan sections

9

environment, service user need, volumes of service commissioned or delivered, costs and performance, etc.

Direction

The purpose of the direction section is to help the reader understand why the service exists, the key objectives and in broad terms how these will be achieved. The content of this section should be reasonably predictable by the reader as they already understand the current and future context for the service.

Action planning

Once the reader has completed the action planning section they should be convinced that the actions proposed are realistic and, if the plan is approved, that they will happen. Typically this section will include information regarding what needs to be done, monitoring arrangements, resource estimates, risk assessments and links to other plans.

What constitutes a good quality plan?

Whether a plan is considered to be of good quality depends to an extent on the views of those receiving it. Typically evaluation criteria include the following components.

1. The plan should be informed by sufficient analysis. All plans should be based on an appropriate level of analysis.
2. The plan should contain actions aimed at achieving the best possible balance of outcomes for different stakeholders. Planning can be challenging in health and social care contexts as different stakeholders may express different needs and wishes, some of which are likely to conflict.
3. The plan should balance short- and long-term outcomes. Often it is possible to achieve positive short-term outcomes at the expense of future generations, for example, by pushing costs into future years. A good plan will, however, consider and balance short- and longer-term outcomes.
4. The plan should be persuasive. Plans are generally prepared in order to persuade others of the wisdom of proposed actions, to secure resources or perhaps permission to significantly change the service. Persuasiveness relies on the quality of the document, the desirability of the planned outcome and the impression given of the ability of those who will deliver the planned actions. A plan which may be excellent in terms of proposed actions may not secure approval because the reader is not persuaded of the wisdom of the approach or assured of the managerial ability of those who will deliver it.
5. The plan should be useful. A good plan will be referred to frequently and is likely to have a 'well-thumbed' look to it.

In a well-managed organisation, the criteria by which plans are evaluated will be known to those involved and developmental feedback given each time a plan is submitted for approval.

Table 2.3 is an example plan evaluation form which includes criteria that explicitly or implicitly inform judgements about plan quality. It should be noted that this example focuses on the quality of the plan rather than the merits of the proposed direction and action.

ACTIVITY 2.2

Plan evaluation

Take a recent plan prepared for your service or organisation and complete the evaluation form provided as Table 2.3.

Which of the following verdicts would you give?

- Approval
- Approval subject to revision
- Approval subject to revision and resubmission
- Rejection, rewriting and resubmission

Identify two aspects of the plan that you consider to be of very good quality or where further development is necessary.

Table 2.3 Plan evaluation form

Plan evaluation form

	Criteria	Explanation	Feedback comments	Development suggestions
1.	Is the plan accessible?	*Is the plan written in a way that can be understood by the intended reader(s)?*		
2.	Does the plan flow?	*Does content regarding the current situation and how this might develop support planned action?*		
3.	Is the plan of appropriate length?	*Given service complexity and the needs of the reader is the plan of appropriate length? If the plan is too short the reader may not have sufficient information for their purposes; too long and they may lose sight of the strategic direction or be put off reading it.*		
4.	Does the plan contain sufficient detail regarding the internal and external context?	*Is there enough detail regarding the service context for the reader to understand whether the actions proposed in a plan are appropriate and feasible?*		
5.	Does the plan appear to be the product of a sound process?	*Has sufficient opportunity and time been given for those with a stake in the service to contribute to the plan?*		

Table 2.3 Continued

Plan evaluation form

	Criteria	Explanation	Feedback comments	Development suggestions
6.	Does the plan show how this links to other plans?	*Is appropriate linkage made to other plans within or outside the organisation?*		
7.	Is the plan self-critical?	*Have weaknesses been identified and evaluated?*		
8.	Does the plan take account of the views of key stakeholders?	*Does the plan appear to be informed by stakeholders? Is there evidence of balancing conflicting priorities and long/short-term perspectives?*		
9.	Does the plan include a clear and justified statement of direction and SMART objectives?	*Does the plan include a broad aim or statement of purpose together with objectives or outcomes that together are Specific, Measurable, Achievable, Realistic and Time-related?*		
10.	Is there evidence that planned performance is being stretched, yet realistic?	*Does it appear that assumptions about the design, delivery and management of the existing service have been challenged, performance levels checked against others and stretch improvements included?*		
11.	Does the plan indicate the level of resources required to support the plan?	*As a minimum does the plan include a broad statement of required resources and budget? Does it appear that more detailed analysis exists elsewhere?*		
12.	Does the plan reassure the reader that planned actions will happen?	*Are the actions required to achieve the plan clear, have responsibilities been assigned and are arrangements for monitoring appropriate?*		
13.	Have risks been considered?	*Have risks been considered, are contingency plans in place and will key variables be monitored?*		

Section 3
The planning process

This section outlines a planning process and suggests a number of key questions to consider when preparing to plan.

The planning process that provides the underlying structure for this section comprises six stages as depicted in Figure 3.1.

Planning stages

The first, and often neglected, stage of the process is *planning to plan* where key questions regarding the whole process should be addressed.

The second, and most important, stage involves three interlocking activities, which mirror the plan format introduced in Section 2 — analysis, direction setting and action planning. This stage should involve a mix of strategic and operational thinking informed by various planning techniques.

The third stage concerns writing the plan document prior to presenting it for approval. It is important during this stage to allow sufficient time for plan contributors to comment on early drafts.

The fourth stage involves presentation, approval and feedback via electronic or paper process.

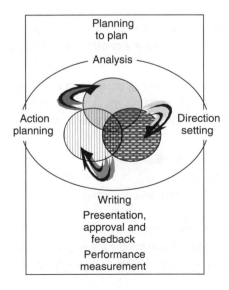

Figure 3.1 The planning process

The penultimate stage sees attention shift to implementation, which involves sustaining ongoing activity whilst engaging in service development.

The final stage of the process involves periodic reporting of progress against plan leading as necessary to management action.

Planning to plan questions

A poor quality planning process can lead to excessive time spent on plan completion, disengaged stakeholders and, ultimately, a poor quality plan document.

A good quality plan is almost inevitably due to there being an effective planning process that can be shaped by answering the questions in Table 3.1.

Table 3.1 Planning to plan – key questions

Key questions	Factors to consider
Who will receive the plan and for what purpose?	The answer to this question helps those writing the plan to tailor the content, style and tone to meet the needs of the reader(s). Where readership is diverse it might be desirable to prepare two or more versions of the plan.
What plan format will be used?	Does a particular format have to be used? If the format is not predetermined, is an existing one suitable or will a new format need to be designed?
Who should be involved in planning, and how?	Plan quality normally benefits from the involvement of a range of people; either as full members of a planning group, attendees at a planning event, as occasional contributors of ideas or draft readers. Different people have different perspectives and may well have information that will prove useful. However, the potential value of this involvement needs to be balanced against the time and cost involved.
What guidance and support will be given to those involved?	All those participating in planning will need to be briefed and for those new to the process it might be necessary to offer some training or other support.
What will be communicated to those not directly involved in planning?	Plan content is potentially of interest to all stakeholders and an early decision is needed about process and content confidentiality; options include total secrecy, regular controlled briefings or open proceedings.
What timetable will be adopted for planning?	The timetable for planning should be influenced by: • the answers to the above questions; • the final deadline for plan submission and any interim organisational deadlines; • peaks and troughs of work, holidays, etc. Planning needs to start earlier where more people are engaged in the process, where the linkage between plans is high or where funding

Table 3.1 Continued

Key questions	Factors to consider
	implications need to feed into the planning and budget cycle of other agencies. However, the earlier the timetable starts the greater the uncertainty about the future – more drafts of the plan will be needed.
What criteria will be used to evaluate the plan?	If the quality of the plan is to continuously improve, it should be evaluated. Those planning should self-assess the quality of the process and the document, and receive developmental feedback from those responsible for plan approval.
How does the plan link with other systems?	Rarely can a plan be prepared in total isolation from other plans in the organisation and prior to planning it is worth identifying: • plans that drive or influence this plan; • plans that are driven or influenced by this plan; • plans that need to directly link with this plan.
Who will write the plan?	While there is a tendency to assume that the most senior person involved in planning should write the document, another member of the planning group might be more appropriate.
Who will present the plan?	If plans are to be presented at a meeting, consideration needs to be given as to whether this should be done by the most senior manager or the 'team'. Giving prominence to a team can demonstrate collective ownership and energy in support of the proposals, and increase reader confidence. However, this outcome will depend on the ability a wider team has to present and deal with questions.

15

Section 4
Using planning techniques

This section describes a number of planning techniques that support the preparation of the three main sections of a plan. Also included are tips for success relating to the use of techniques.

Introduction

A person who plans without analysis and strategic thought has little option but to base their decisions about the future on what has previously been done, on what others are doing, intuition or whim.

A good quality plan is the product of strategic thought which benefits from the conscious use of planning techniques, each of which offers a framework for gathering and arranging information or thoughts in a way that increases service understanding and leads to valuable insights.

In practice, many plans appear to be informed by only two well-established techniques – (1) an environmental scan, and (2) a strengths, weaknesses, opportunities and threats (SWOT) analysis. These techniques can be very helpful and various questions or checklists exist to support their use (Semple Piggot (2000) and Mintzberg *et al.* (1998)). However, while these techniques can yield valuable information there is a danger of over-familiarity and lack of rigour. The outcome of a SWOT analysis in particular can be superficial due to the common practice of presenting it in bullet point form using a neat four-cell grid, all on one page of a flip chart.

Over the years a number of other techniques have become available to planners that can add considerable value to the planning process. These techniques vary in sophistication, the time required to use them and cost; some can be used in almost all contexts while others need to be used selectively and/or tweaked.

The techniques explained in this section tend to be relatively simple, cost effective and generally applicable.

To gain maximum benefit from the use of planning techniques, a number of factors should be considered, as captured in the following tips for success.

Completing the analysis

This section poses seven questions, the answers to which form the basis of the analysis section of a plan:

1. What do we know about our performance?
2. What do we know about how we operate?
3. What do we know about the environment?
4. What do we know about those that use our services and the services we provide or commission?
5. What do we know about others that provide similar services?
6. What do we know about opportunities and threats?
7. What restraints affect our planning?

1. What do we know about our performance?

The answer to this question helps the reader understand recent and current levels of achievement, should lead to successes being recognised and celebrated, stimulates organisational learning and provides information for assessing the desirability and feasibility of proposed actions.

There are three main ways of considering performance.

1. By comparing actual and planned performance which results in understanding of the extent to which objectives have been met, or are being met. It also highlights part achieved or wholly unachieved objectives which might need to be included in the plan now being prepared.
2. By comparing performance over the last few years which helps those planning to see patterns and trends in key areas.
3. By comparison with similar services and organisations which provides a sense of relative performance and may indicate areas where there is scope for potential improvement.

Where there is a current approved plan this may include a mix of objectives, some that feature every year (for example, to 'keep within approved budget') and others which are one off in nature (for example, to 'introduce a new accounting system by 1 April 20XX'). Performance in respect of both types of objectives should be reported in the plan.

Where an existing plan is available the following questions can help when reviewing performance.

1. What key objectives are included in the current plan? A key objective is one where non-achievement or part-achievement would have serious implications.
2. What performance targets are included in the current plan?
3. What is the current level of performance?
4. Where current levels of performance differ from target, what are the main reasons?
5. How has actual performance changed over the last three years and why?
6. How does performance compare to other organisations and why?
7. Is there any additional evidence available to support performance claims?
8. Have any new performance targets become important during the year, e.g. a new national performance indicator?

If this is the first time that a plan is being prepared questions 1) and 2) should be replaced with the following.

1. What aspects of performance do you currently measure and what targets apply? These performance measures may be evident from organisational documents, inferred from the behaviours of leaders and other stakeholders, etc.

    Or, otherwise:

2. Taking account of national, organisational and local perspectives, what do you consider to be important measures for your service and reasonable target performance levels?

Table 4.1 can be used to capture performance information. It should be noted that the first time a plan is prepared it is common for performance information to be missing – where this occurs this should be recorded as a 'weakness' and lead to action in the 'direction' section. For some types of objectives it is not relevant to look at performance over time, or against other organisations, and in these instances some of the columns will remain blank.

Depending on the circumstances described earlier, planned or desirable levels of performance should be entered in column 2, current performance in column 3 and the difference between these in column 4. Where appropriate, column 5 can be completed to show how performance is changing over time and column 6 where it is possible to compare performance with other organisations. The final column can be used to record sources of additional evidence or comment on the performance measure.

2. What do we know about how we operate?

Critical to maintaining or improving performance is understanding how different aspects of service operation affect current performance.

One technique for developing this understanding is a strengths and weaknesses analysis, the aim of which is to identify current:

- strengths that contribute to success and alert the reader to any action needed to preserve or enhance these;
- weaknesses that adversely affect performance and which if left unaddressed pose significant future risks to the service.

Table 4.1 Performance analysis

Objectives	Planned or desired level	Actual current level	Gap (Column 2–3) and reasons	Over time is performance: * Constant? * Improving? * Weakening?	Compared to other services	Evidence or comment
1	2	3	4	5	6	7
Reduce average gross hourly cost of home help/carer	£15.50	£15.80	30p per hour higher than planned	Improving given that last year this was £16.90	Relevant national average – £15.00	Although higher than planned, and higher than the average, this is lower than last year
Staff opinion survey (improved overall satisfaction levels)	85%	79%	6% lower than planned	Constant	Not applicable	A major reorganisation and irritation with the main computer system has impacted negatively
Introduce new Management Information System	£100,000 By 30/11/11	£105,400 By 01/02/12	£5,400 overspend 2 months late	Not applicable	Not applicable	Unforeseen problems with electrical supply
Achieve year on year efficiency savings	2%	2.9%	0.9% better than planned	Improving	Not known	No comment

It should be noted that strengths and weaknesses are often combined with external opportunities and threats to become a strengths, weaknesses, opportunities and threats (SWOT) analysis. While many planners use SWOT, there is a case for separating strengths and weaknesses from opportunities and threats. Separation makes analysis easier and often leads to deeper consideration and better understanding. The opportunities and threats analysis is usually better completed later in the planning process when more is known about the environment, market, alternative providers etc.

While a strengths and weaknesses analysis is relatively straightforward to complete, material relating to this in plans is often quite poor. While this is sometimes due to presentation, more often it appears to be due to a failure to undertake the analysis in a sufficiently rigorous way, leading to plan content that:

- is simply a list of bullet points, the meaning of which may be unclear to the reader;
- includes strengths and weaknesses which appear irrelevant or of only minor importance;
- is generalised and of limited value, e.g. 'our staff' recorded as a strength implies that every single member of staff is a strength and in every respect;
- includes asserted strengths which managers would like to believe but which are not necessarily true;
- contains little indication as to whether each strength or weakness is growing or reducing in significance;
- offers little indication as to whether claimed strengths and weaknesses are common to other providers of this service;
- includes only strengths and weaknesses generated by those planning rather than those that might be identified by other staff, managers, service users, etc.

In order to ensure maximum value is derived from the analysis a three-stage process is suggested, as shown in the steps below.

Step 1
Plan the process by which strengths and weaknesses are to be identified, analysed and assessed.

Step 2
Record strengths and weaknesses on a grid such as the one appearing as Table 4.2, ensuring that:

- each strength or weakness is recorded in sufficient detail to make it specific;
- the impact of the strength or weakness on the service is clearly described;
- the significance of the impact of each strength and weakness is indicated using low, medium and high classifications;
- an indication is given of whether in respect of identified strengths and weaknesses this service or organisation is better or worse than others;
- an indication is given of whether the importance of each strength or weakness is decreasing, static or increasing;
- any evidence to support the claimed strength or weakness is stated.

Step 3
Decide which strengths or weaknesses should be included in the plan by selecting those that will need to be built on later. For example, if the plan records as a weakness 'the quality of

Table 4.2 Strengths and weaknesses analysis – an example

Strengths/ weaknesses	How this impacts on the service	Significance (high, low, medium)	Is it a relative strength or weakness?	Increasing, decreasing or static?	Evidence
Strengths					
High percentage of staff with a managerial qualification	Exceeds external expectations regarding qualifications levels. Likely positive affect on the quality of managers and therefore management which should positively impact on staff morale, care quality and performance	Medium	Relative strength – a lot of similar organisations are struggling to meet even minimum levels	Static, having grown over the last three years	Quantitative information regarding numbers qualified. Positive inspection comments. However, no evidence to support the link between qualifications and performance
Weaknesses					
Computer Equipment	Equipment is old, slow and crashes – service users do not get the service they should and staff time is wasted	High	Suspect other services have better equipment	Increasing problem	Staff and customer surveys have both cited computer systems as being poor

information regarding the future cost of care packages' the reader will rightly expect to see an objective addressing this in the direction section. While reported strengths may not demand any particular action, the reader should appreciate how these contribute to performance.

3. What do we know about the environment?

This question prompts consideration about the environment within in which the service operates, how this might change in the future and the implications for the service.

The process by which this information is gathered, analysed and interpreted is known as environmental analysis, the intended outcome of which is not a precise prediction of the future; rather, a general sense of how the environment might develop, key themes and major challenges. A good quality environmental scan indicates that those planning are engaging externally and taking into account short- and long-term perspectives. The frameworks involved in environmental analysis help those planning to tackle its difficult nature, in particular the diversity of influences and interconnectedness, or complexity. The outcome of this analysis is likely to be more strategic thinking and a better document than would otherwise be the case.

The literature regarding strategy and planning features a number of approaches to environmental scanning, central to which tend to be acronyms such as PEST and PESTEL. These acronyms provide a framework for the planner to identify environmental influences that are, for example, political, economic or sociological in nature.

The following approach to environmental analysis recognises five major sources of external influence: sociological, political, economic, legal and technological (SPELT). Consideration of environmental factors should take into account three timeframes: 1) influences that are impacting now; 2) those expected to impact within three years; and 3) those that might impact beyond three years, as indicated in Figure 4.1.

Environmental scanning involves four stages; influence identification, impact assessment, action and reporting.

The first stage is to identify key environment influences that are affecting the service now or are likely to in future; these are likely to include some that affect:

- society in general, as well as the service being planned, e.g. increasing life expectancy and the implications this has for the level and length of care required;
- the health and social care sector generally and which impact on the service, e.g. a shortage of nursing staff and the implications this will have for agency use, recruitment, employment practice, costs, etc.;

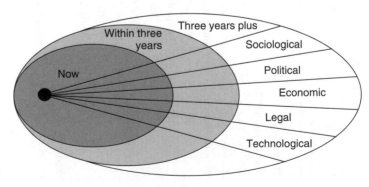

Figure 4.1 SPELT analysis

- the organisation specifically and which also impact on the service, for example, a decision to build a new housing estate and the implications this has for service demand, capacity levels and service location.

It should be noted that influences often relate to two or more categories. It does not matter which category an influence is recorded against – what is important is that it is captured and considered. The purpose of the five classifications is to prompt, not limit, thinking.

Table 4.3 indicates some significant environmental influences relating to a service specialising in treating liver disease.

Impact assessment

The second stage of the environmental scan is to assess each influence using the following questions.

1. In what way is this environmental influence likely to affect activities and/or operations?
2. How significant will the impact of this influence be for the service?
3. What is the probability that this degree of impact will be experienced?

For many planners this assessment is reasonably straightforward as can be seen in Table 4.3. In more complex situations preparing an issues priority matrix such as that advocated by Luffman *et al.* (1987: 28) can be helpful.

Action

Having identified the key influences the planner should, as appropriate:

1. Examine these influences in detail whilst this plan is being prepared and propose action where necessary.
2. Decide to investigate these influences in greater detail during the period covered by the plan.
3. Report in the plan that no immediate action is required but that the environmental influence will be monitored. This can be appropriate where the influence is not currently strong but could become so or because the impact is sufficiently in the future that action at this stage is considered unnecessary.

Reporting

To keep the length of the main body of the plan reasonably detailed, material resulting from the environmental analysis should be included as an appendix. The main text of the plan should simply include:

- a general statement of how the future is seen, for example,

  'the future is likely to see a continued increase in alcohol-related illness and a greater range of more technical expensive medical treatments becoming available coinciding with significantly reduced budgets.'

  And

- any specific points you wish to draw to the attention of the reader, where you believe action is required, for example,

  'Of concern is the ever increasing difficulty of attracting staff given other health employment opportunities in the region and the relatively poor remuneration package.'

Table 4.3 SPELT influences – an example

Categories	Example environmental influences	Possible implications – (related to a liver unit)
Sociological	Population growth and composition, morbidity, mortality, life style choices, trends in housing, care expectations, etc.	e.g. General increase in consumption of alcohol combined with changes in drinking patterns and habits. *High impact and high probability*
Political	Key policies at European, national, regional and local levels – changes in spending priorities, shifts in thinking about organisational forms and operation, etc.	e.g. Changes to paternity rights and entitlements. *Low impact and high probability*
Economic	Key economic trends including employment, growth, inflation, interest rates, government spending, central and local taxation.	e.g. Severe recession will lead to several years of significant cuts in public funding. *High impact and high probability*
Legal	Legislation that is either general, for example, relating to employment and health and safety, or specific to services, service users or organisations covered by the plan. Coverage would also include draft legislation.	e.g. Attempts to reduce demand for alcohol by controlling prices and special offers. *Low impact and high probability*
Technological	Includes developments in care practice and management, patient treatment, new ways of working, medical equipment, information systems, computer equipment, etc.	e.g. Potential advances in the treatment of liver conditions. *Moderate impact and medium probability*

4. What do we know about those that use our services and the services we provide or commission?

As organisational plans significantly affect service users, consideration of their needs should influence service direction and, therefore, feature in plans. However, it is surprisingly common to come across plans that make little or no reference to service users, their needs or current levels of satisfaction.

In the private sector it has long been recognised that understanding customers is vital to success and much has been written about the importance of retaining customers, encouraging repeat purchasing and attracting new customers. However, for many public and voluntary sector organisations, creating and maintaining demand is not a problem – on the contrary, demand appears almost limitless as do customer or service user expectations. The combination of limited resources and limitless demand exerts pressure on managers to increase service volume and drive down unit costs. However, this can compromise quality to the extent that the service has little or no value. Irrespective of service volumes or low unit costs a service that does not satisfy the needs of service users is unlikely to represent value for money.

Irrespective of sector it is vital to understand and respond to service users – this involves:

- deciding which service users should be targeted to receive a service;
- identifying service user needs for each target group and deciding which are to be met;
- designing and delivering services that address service user needs at an acceptable cost.

Service users are rarely a homogenous group; in practice they comprise sub-groups, or segments, each sufficiently different as to merit separate attention. In the not-for-profit sector a key decision relates to which users should receive a service, or at least which group(s) the service should primarily be aimed at. Where the service is aimed at more than one sub-group, a further decision is required regarding the extent to which this should be tailored. Service tailoring should lead to levels of satisfaction that are higher than where a 'one size fits all' approach is adopted.

There is no universal way of grouping service users; this depends on context. Common examples include grouping by age, gender and need. A profile is needed for each group; this involves gathering information considered useful by those planning. Table 4.4 indicates some of the information that can be useful.

Table 4.4 is appropriate where there is one service and a number of sub-groups. However, many situations involve multiple services and multiple user groups, in which case the analysis is more complex. In these situations, either this can be replicated for each service or one used which brings together services and groups in respect of a particular piece of information. An example of this latter grid can be seen in Table 4.5 which shows where money is currently spent in terms of a portfolio of services and four user groups.

Table 4.4 Service user summary

Service user information	Group A	Group B	Group C	Total
Description and characteristics of each group	Under 11 years	11–17	18 plus	
Number of current service users	1,097	562	3,490	5,149
Estimated number of future service users – next year	1,200	650	3,720	5,570
Units of service currently consumed (hours)	32,800	17,890	65,400	116,090
Trends in service usage	Slow Increase	Slow Increase	Slow Decrease	
Pattern of use (e.g. frequency, length of use, timing, etc.)	Etc.	Etc.	Etc.	
Identified needs	Etc.	Etc.	Etc.	

Gathering service user information is challenging, however, the questions or insights this generates often prove valuable when looking at factors such as patterns of demand and resource allocation. Table 4.5, for example, shows that:

1. £136,500 of the budget (87%) is spent on Service B.
2. £67,500 of the budget (43%) is spent with service users in Group D.
3. Service users in Group D and receiving Service B account for £60,000 of the total budget (38%).

Table 4.5 Service/user analysis grid

	Group A	Group B	Group C	Group D	Total of all Groups
Service A	£1,000	£12,000	£0	£500	£13,500
Service B	£24,500	£32,000	£20,000	£60,000	£136,500
Service C	£0	£0	£0	£7,000	£7,000
Total Service	£25,500	£44,000	£20,000	£67,500	£157,000

In isolation, this information is interesting but not necessarily useful. However, if this were combined with information regarding service user activity it would be possible to identify items such as unit costs, average spend per service user, etc.

This grid can incorporate historic/current information or illustrate how the future might look taking account of anticipated changes in the environment identified using a SPELT analysis, as explained earlier.

Central to a well developed understanding of service users is the extent to which their needs or wants are known. In this context a *need* is defined as being something which is essential to a service user whereas a *want* is a way of expressing something a service user would like. Taking, for example, a visit to the dentist, a patient might say they 'want an injection' whereas they actually 'need to avoid treatment pain'. Recognising the need rather than the want allows the dentist to consider other ways of minimising or avoiding treatment pain which might be in addition to, or even instead of, an injection.

Needs and wants are often confused and those planning should focus on the former. Identifying and responding to needs rather than wants is good practice as a service user may say they want something out of habit or because they simply cannot imagine anything else being possible. How a want is expressed may be quite different from the underlying need from which this flows and understanding the latter can significantly change service providers' thinking about clients and services. Failure to do this may leave a need unaddressed, or only partially addressed, with satisfaction levels lower than might otherwise be anticipated.

With services led by professional staff there is a temptation to design and deliver based on norms set by experts. These normative needs may lag behind changes in the environment and fail to reflect current aspirations of service users

The importance of distinguishing between wants and needs is illustrated in Table 4.6, which relates to a coach company offering a programme of days out for retired, relatively fit and reasonably wealthy people living in a particular town. The company has a clear target user group in terms of age, catchment area and disposable income; a user group which they have served for many years. It is easy for planners to assume that because service users continue to purchase a service they must be satisfied and, therefore, the future of the service is secure. However, continued use might simply be due to there being few alternatives or users purchasing from habit. If at any point choice becomes available, personal habit is interrupted, environmental change occurs or customer expectations alter, demand might suddenly fall. Those planning need to know how satisfied their customers are, the underlying reasons for this level of satisfaction and whether this is rising or falling. This knowledge will ultimately indicate the scope for increasing satisfaction levels through changing service design and, or, operation.

Being aware that a need exists does not mean that a service provider has to address it; a decision often has to be made as to which needs a service will address and equally those it will

Table 4.6 Wants and needs of customers of a coach company offering day trips

Expressed wants	Felt needs
I want a nice seat with a headrest.	I need to feel comfortable.
I want to be dropped at the end of my road.	I need to feel safe from personal attack when I get back home.
I want a reasonable number and length of stops during a journey.	I need to feel comfortable and relaxed about the length of time I will have to wait for the next stop. I need not to feel rushed or anxious about missing the bus when taking a break.
I don't want to be thrown about when we go round corners.	I need to be safe and feel safe in the coach.
I want to be able to get on and off the coach easily.	I need to be able to do things for myself.

not. Likewise, a decision is often required regarding the extent to which an identified need is met.

In this example, many needs are present, their relative importance varying from person to person. Each person identifies and prioritises needs differently and, in effect, has a personal balance of need for which they seek satisfaction. For the service provider, different personal balances of need can be difficult to accommodate. In the coach example, if the need to feel comfortable and safe is responded to it will probably increase costs and, ultimately, price – which some users will be prepared to pay. However, other users may be more interested in a low price, even if a degree of comfort and safety is sacrificed. Where different balances of need exist, those planning could consider:

- focusing exclusively on a selected group(s), in the coach example perhaps specialising in a rather more luxurious service where customers are dropped at the end of their road;
- compromising and accepting that some people from both groups are likely to be less than fully satisfied; for some, the service is a 'bit expensive' while for others it is a 'bit uncomfortable and uncaring';
- designing services that separately fulfil the needs of two or more sub-groups.

Continuing with the coach example, it would be quite easy to respond to a customer who *wants* to be dropped off at the end of their road. However, this is simply how the customer articulates the deeper need 'to feel safe from personal attack when they get back home'. The company could decide to more fully address this need by dropping each customer at their door and ensuring they safely enter their house before driving off. Clearly, there would be operational and cost implications associated with this level of service which some customers would find acceptable; others would not.

Knowledge of service user need helps those planning to decide which needs to address, to generate ideas to meet these and understand the implications this has for service design and operation. Table 4.7 develops the previous example by identifying three user wants, needs and some of the ingredients of service design and operation which the provider may employ in order to increase satisfaction.

Table 4.7 Wants, needs and ingredients

Expressed wants	Felt needs	Provider ingredients
I want a nice seat with a headrest.	I need to feel comfortable.	Seat design, layout leg/head room, tray rests, individual lights, curtains, air flow, etc.
I want to be dropped at the end of my road.	I need to feel safe from personal attack when I get back home.	Drop off arrangements.
I want a reasonable number and length of stops during a journey.	I need to feel comfortable and relaxed about the length of time I will have to wait for the next stop. I need not to feel rushed or anxious about missing the bus when taking a break.	Journey planning and publication of planned stops. Clearly announced length of stops. Headcounts before departure. Sufficient time to visit the toilet and have light refreshments, etc. On board toilets, drinks, etc.

Identifying, selecting and meeting the needs of those users intended to receive a service is key to long-term profitability in the private sector and to best value elsewhere. As far as possible, the felt needs of the service user should match the features of the service offered. The shape in the middle of the Venn diagram in Figure 4.2 represents the extent to which felt need is being met by the service. Segment A, to the left of the diagram, shows unmet felt need. Segment B represents features that are part of the service but which do not meet identified service user needs. As features cost money to incorporate in the service they should be deleted unless specifically relevant to service user need, required by statute or required to meet the needs of other stakeholders.

Best value is achieved through:

a) avoiding, where possible, including service features that users do not need, particularly where these incur cost to the provider;
b) identifying important needs which, if met, would increase the net value of the service;
c) identifying and targeting resources to particular groups, each with their own characteristic balance of needs.

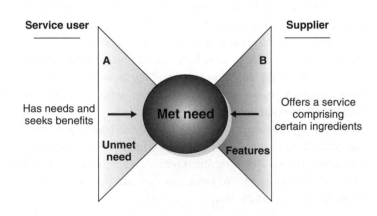

Figure 4.2 Needs and features – Venn diagram

Understanding the needs of service users enables the provider to target the most appropriate group(s), to be clear about the needs the service will meet (and how well they will be met) and to organise and behave in a way that is likely to meet need and maximise user satisfaction.

While poor service in the private sector may result in falling sales and reduced profit, elsewhere service users may continue to consume a service, particularly if it is free, simply because it is all that there is on offer.

A further characteristic of some not-for-profit sector organisations is that users are sometimes required to receive a service they do not want. However, even where choice regarding consumption has to be denied there will be other user needs that a good service provider should seek to meet.

It should be noted that success involves more than meeting just service user needs – frequently there are a range of other stakeholders, each with their own needs, which may coincide, overlap or contradict those expressed by service users. A good plan will identify, balance and prioritise the needs of all stakeholders.

The final part of service user analysis is to bring together the needs of the service user, assess the extent to which the current service meets these and identify the scope for better tailoring. Table 4.8 shows how a simple service assessment grid can be used to capture this information, in this instance relating to a GP Surgery.

5. What do we know about others that provide similar services?

Irrespective of sector, planning processes benefit from knowledge about how the service or organisation compares with other, similar ones. Private sector companies providing similar services are usually to some degree in competition and planners need to understand as much as possible about competitors in order to find an 'edge'. For organisations operating without a profit motive the term 'alternative provider' rather than competitor can feel more appropriate, although it should be noted that whilst not perhaps competing for customers they may be competing for league table position, funding, good quality staff, political support, etc.

The challenge here is to identify alternative providers that are similar, could be competing and are high performing. The following questions provide a framework for starting to gather, sort and interpret information about an alternative provider.

Two problems exist when looking at alternative providers; firstly getting one or more suitable organisations to share information can be difficult due to confidentiality, time and cost concerns. The more competitive the relationship, the less likely that information sharing will be possible. Secondly, the quality of information can be variable and in practice those planning frequently have to rely on published sources or information gleaned at conferences, from contacts, and so on.

While alternative provider analysis might be difficult to undertake and there may be concerns regarding information reliability, this is still worthwhile. It should be noted that in the early years of planning, understanding about other providers is usually limited and rather anecdotal but this can be developed over time.

Table 4.8 Service assessment grid

Service user needs	How needs are addressed by service features	Current shortfalls	Improvement suggestions
To avoid sitting in the surgery for a long time when feeling ill.	For emergency appointments, patients are asked to join the end of the morning list.	If there are a lot of emergency patients, some have to wait for more than an hour to see a doctor.	Give emergency patients an approximate appointment time when they book.
To know they can park their cars safely and not have to drive round for ages before walking a long way to the surgery.	A large car park at nearby shops.	At busy times the shop car park is full and patients cannot find a space.	Little possibility of improvement in the short term – could make the use of public transport and taxis as easy as possible – leaflets, telephone numbers, etc.
To feel they are valued as a person.	By the way in which receptionists, nurses and doctors talk to patients.	No known shortfalls.	None proposed.
To feel relaxed in the waiting area.	Provision of reading matter, comfortable chairs, clear signage, adequate PA system, etc.	Poor PA system – can be unclear as to which patient has been called. Patients are often confused as to which waiting room they should go to.	Upgrade PA system, invest in loop facility and improve signage to consulting rooms.
To avoid having to take time off work to attend non-urgent appointments.	Practice is currently open until 6.30 p.m. on weekday evenings.	Patients who work away from home or in London have to take time off work to attend surgery.	Open later one night a week and start a Saturday morning surgery.

Table 4.9 Alternative provider framework

Aspect	Comment
What services do they offer?	This will help identify the range of services and the extent to which another organisation might be comparable.
How large are they?	Knowing the volume of service, number of clients, financial turnover, full-time equivalent staff, etc., helps determine whether another organisation is comparable in terms of scale.
Who funds, or purchases from, them?	This helps to identify whether an alternative provider needs to 'win' income and, if so, from where – this may help with assessing their level of vulnerability regarding sources of funding/income and deciding whether the organisation is likely to be competing.
Where is their market place?	This should establish if an alternative provider is operating in the same market which might mean that they are competing for users, funders, etc.
Is anything known about their future intentions?	This might be gleaned from statements in the press regarding new services/new facilities and possible competitive activity, etc.
Why do those that use their service do so?	This will help with understanding what makes other organisations attractive to their service users – possible scope for replication.
How financially healthy are they?	Using published accounts can help understanding regarding financial performance and how this compares.
What do we know about them?	This concerns how the organisation is structured and operates; quality of buildings, staff numbers, pay and conditions, marketing, etc. This might yield ideas for potential improvement.

TIPS FOR SUCCESS

- *When identifying services/organisations for comparison, make sure they are similar to your own and likely to be competing.*
- *Select organisations that are considered 'high' performers.*
- *Assign responsibility for gathering published information about selected organisations to members of the management team.*
- *Create a central reference point for storing alternative provider information as it is acquired.*
- *Consider whether comparison should be taken a step further and benchmarking considered.*

6. What do we know about opportunities and threats?

Identifying, understanding and responding to opportunities and threats when planning is vital as this can prompt service development, growth and performance improvement as well as protect against potential problems.

Four questions provide a framework for addressing opportunities and threats.

1. What are the main opportunities and threats facing the service over the next few years?
2. What is the potential impact of each opportunity or threat?
3. How significant is the likely impact of each opportunity or threat?
4. What is the likelihood that the potential impact will occur?

The starting point is to review the outcome of all the analysis to date and identify any significant opportunities and threats. These might relate to factors identified earlier, for example, through an environmental scan, or could be the result of the interplay of different factors, for example, an environmental influence combined with a change in identified service user needs.

As this analysis can result in a long list of potential opportunities and threats these should be assessed for significance and likelihood with the important ones included in the body of the plan. Table 4.10 is a framework for considering opportunities and threats, in this example relating to budget pressure on a children's service.

Table 4.10 Opportunities and threats analysis

Opportunity/ threat	Potential impact	Potential significance (Score 1–10 where 10 is high)	Likelihood of Occurrence (Score 1–10 where 10 is high)	Possible responses
1	2	3	4	5
Threat 1. Pressure on budgets relating to children and young people associated with the recession and the continued drive for efficiency in local government.	Children's services are likely to be increasingly in the 'spotlight', and significant cuts will be required. A rolling programme of reviews and increased with member scrutiny likely.	8	9	Develop cost information Review high cost service areas Undertake comparison with other authorities Link plans and budgets Help portfolio members develop their appreciation of the service

The proposed approach uses a scale of 1 to 10, where 1 is low and 10 is high, to explain the potential significance of the threat and the likelihood that it will occur.

The first column is used to describe the identified opportunities and threats; the second describes the potential impact on the service. Columns 3 and 4 record the significance and likelihood scores. Where the opportunity or threat looks significant, column 5 should be completed, describing possible responses.

Without an opportunities and threats analysis, planners might fail to receive early warning of a potential opportunity or threat and, regarding the scenario in Table 4.10, might only become aware of a budget problem when local politicians and or strategic managers start to implement cuts, reviews, etc.

7. What restraints affect our planning?

Most plans relate to part of an organisation rather than the whole, and those planning are rarely free to do what they wish, however compelling they may consider their case. Plans, and the actions they contain, usually have to be approved by senior managers, trustees and/or politicians, each of whom will have their own view as to the purpose of the service and how it should operate.

A plan that fails to reflect the requirements and preferences of significant stakeholders is likely to be rejected. In effect, a set of restraints exist which affect aspects of the service including potentially target service users, purpose, organisational structure and operation.

Identifying restraints, or 'givens' as they are sometimes referred to, can be difficult as these may not exist in writing and are implicit, perhaps linked to a particular incident in the past. Restraints are often deeply embedded and can seriously limit thinking, so it is vital that those planning know the restraints within which they are expected to operate, and are prepared to challenge these when necessary.

If the restraints are not clear planners have three main options:

1. Ask senior managers, politicians, trustees, etc., to clearly state the restraints that should be observed.
2. State in the plan the restraints the stakeholders believe exist so that those approving the document are aware that these have affected the proposed direction and planned actions.
3. Plan without regard to restraints but be prepared for the document to be rejected and the planning process extended.

If any identified restraints are considered inappropriate, or unduly limiting, those planning should consider:

- challenging the restraint during the planning process;
- making the recommendations they wish in the plan, even where these run contrary to restraints;
- making the removal or lessening of a restraint an objective in the plan.

And by this point . . .

By the time those reading a plan have come to the end of the analysis section they should have a good understanding of the environment, the unit and service etc., and how these are expected to change over the period covered by the plan. A short summary of the analysis section can help ensure the reader understands what you want them to prior to considering the direction proposed for this service.

Setting direction

The second main section of a plan focuses on the direction of the service, the aim being to inform the reader as to why the service exists, what it is intended to achieve over the life of the plan and the high level actions intended to bring this about.

This clarity is achieved by addressing three key questions:

1. Why do we exist or act as we do?
2. What do we want to achieve?
3. How will we achieve what we want?

The terminology used to describe the why, what and how of direction varies according to organisational practice, personal preference and context, as indicated in Table 4.11.

The content of the direction section of the plan should flow from the earlier analysis and contain no surprises for the reader; nor should it leave any previously raised issues unaddressed. As an example, any weakness considered important enough to be reported in the analysis section of a plan should lead to action in the direction section.

1. Why do we exist or act as we do?

This question is designed to elicit the purpose of the organisation, unit or service. Answering this question can be surprisingly difficult, particularly in respect of a long-established unit where the original reason for the service may have disappeared or those planning have never discussed purpose.

Many planners choose to answer this question with a succinct statement that captures the essence of the organisation or service. However, short statements can be bland and generalised, being little more than a slogan or strapline. Other planners prefer more developed statements but run the risk that these lack clarity and impact.

In practice, there are some situations where a shorter statement is useful and others where a more developed one is needed. A logical response to this dual need is to write a longer statement that includes a succinct expression of purpose.

The length and style of a purpose statement should take into account history, context, leadership style and how the statement is to be used. A matter-of-fact, realistic approach might be appreciated by some commercial stakeholders but is less likely to motivate staff. A deeper, more romantic style might inspire some staff while others may take great delight in pointing out instances where actions or behaviour are inconsistent with the statement.

Table 4.11 Alternative expressions of direction

Section	Common terminology
Why?	e.g. mission, aim, purpose, values, vision
What?	e.g. objectives, outcomes, goals, targets
How?	e.g. strategies, actions

Different forms of statement tend to start with a characteristic phrase; for example, one regarding home care might start with:

'The aim of the home care service is to...'
'Our mission is to be...'
'We have a vision for home care, for a service that...'
'We believe that those that use our home care service...'

The quotation in Figure 4.3 shows how, for a home care service, purpose might be stated using an 'aim' format:

The questions included in Table 4.12 should be considered prior to preparing a statement of purpose.

The process by which a purpose statement will be prepared should be considered carefully and should take into account available time and resources. A suggested process is included as Table 4.13.

Drafting a 'good statement' requires those involved to be clear about what they do and don't stand for, value, provide, etc. As an ultimately convergent process this can be particularly

'We aim to provide a range of tailored services to users in a way that promotes their independence, secures improved quality of life and helps them remain in their own homes.'

Figure 4.3 Example purpose statement

Table 4.12 Preparing a purpose statement – questions

Questions	Consideration
1. How is the statement to be used?	In addition to being part of the plan, the statement might also be used for external communication, aligning staff to service aims, etc.
2. What format is to be used?	Will an aim, mission, vision, belief statement etc. be used to express purpose?
3. What style of writing should be adopted?	Purpose statements can be written in a variety of styles, including: • In a relatively factual and, some would say, cold way, as in *'The purpose of the service is to . . .'* • More powerfully and with conviction, as in *'Our mission is to eradicate . . .'* • In a deeper, more personal way, as in *'We believe in choice, in inclusion, in respect and in all that we do we model these beliefs . . .'*
4. How long do you want the statement to be?	The chosen length of statement should primarily reflect how it is to be used.

35

Table 4.13 Generating a purpose statement – process

Stage	Comment
1. Decide the purpose, format, style and length of desired statement.	This stage involves addressing the key questions outlined in Table 4.12.
2. Identification of themes, issues, ideas or words that should inform a purpose statement.	In the earlier home care example (Figure 4.3) the key elements were: • tailored services; • independence; • quality of life; • remaining in their own homes. Each word or phrase suggests a value, a focus or a way of behaving that is considered important. As identifying, selecting and agreeing key terms can be quite difficult, sufficient time should be allowed for debate.
3. Generation of alternative purpose statements.	Generate a number of alternative statements.
4. Selection of preferred draft statements and review.	Reduce the range and number of statements through an initial discussion and then review selected ones to ensure that: • 'weak' words or phrases such as 'like to', 'might' and 'within the resources available' are replaced with more positive ones such as 'we will'. Positively phrased statements are usually clearer, more motivational and communicate determination; • each statement is consistent with the earlier analysis and that the purpose is appropriate, realistic and desirable.
5. Initial testing, revision and selection of preferred statement(s).	Ask a small number of trusted colleagues to scrutinise preferred statements and challenge the content. Revise statements as appropriate.
6. Wider testing and final drafting	Subject the revised statements to scrutiny by a wider group of key stakeholders prior to final drafting and publication.

uncomfortable when the emerging direction differs from that preferred by one or more of those involved in planning. It is important to allow appropriate time for issues and concerns to be discussed otherwise the final statement may not be owned by key stakeholders.

2. What do we want to achieve?

Having understood the broad purpose of an organisation, unit or service the reader then needs to understand what those planning intend to achieve over the period covered by the plan.

The answer to the question 'What do we want to achieve?' should be in sufficient detail for the reader to feel able to start reaching a judgement regarding approval.

The 'what' of planning can be expressed in a number of ways, for example, as objectives, goals, targets, measures, indicators and outcomes. Please note that for ease of presentation purposes, 'objective' is used to describe how the 'what' of planning is expressed throughout this section.

Objectives tend to fall into two main types:

1. those that are likely to feature in successive plans, for example 'keeping within the agreed budget'; and
2. those that appear in a plan for one year only, for example 'to reduce short-term sickness to X days per person per year' or 'introduce a new human resource information system by...' Once realised, one-off objectives should disappear from future plans.

A good 'what' section helps the reader understand what it is intended to achieve, facilitates effective management and forms the basis of rigorous performance reporting.

Sadly, many plans include objectives that are of poor quality in that they are not specific, measurable, achievable, realistic and timed. An objective to 'reduce annual costs by 5 per cent' might initially look clear and measurable but further examination raises a number of questions, including:

- Which costs are to be reduced? All costs or some costs?
- Is the reduction based on the amount spent last year, the current budget or on some other basis?
- Does this apply in year one of the plan, by the end of the plan or even each year of the plan?

A better expression of this objective is:

To reduce gross revenue spending by 5 per cent in real terms year on year taking the 20XX/XX approved budget as the start point.

A suggested process for deriving objectives can be seen in Table 4.14.

When stating the 'what' of planning, a number of common traps need to be avoided, for example, obscuring the strategic direction by including numerous operational objectives. Such traps can be avoided by observing the following tips for success.

Table 4.14 Deriving objectives

---

1. Decide how to express the 'what' of planning (as objectives, outcomes, goals, etc.)
2. Identify ongoing and important one-off objectives arising from the earlier analysis.
3. Express the objectives in SMART terms (Specific, Measurable, Achievable, Realistic and Timed).
4. Test the objectives to see that they:
   a) Are of primary importance in that failing to achieve these would pose serious risk to clients, the viability of the service, etc.
   b) Fit the organisational givens and are consistent with the purpose statement.
   c) Flow from the earlier analysis.

---

3. How will we achieve what we want?

Although by this point the reader should understand the purpose of the service and the primary objectives, they will not know how it is intended to achieve these or be reassured that these will actually happen.

Normally, a considerable number of actions are necessary to maintain and develop a service over the life of a plan. In order to maintain the strategic focus, it is important that at this stage the planner includes only key actions required to achieve the objectives. More detailed actions will appear in the action planning section and still more in operational plans that flow from this plan. This section should only capture the 'headline' actions intended to deliver the primary objectives.

A simple table such as Table 4.15 is all that is needed; this shows the high level actions intended to achieve each objective.

Table 4.15 High level action summary

Objectives	High level actions
1. To reduce gross revenue spending by 5% in real terms year on year, taking the 20XX/XX approved budget as the start point.	Start a rolling programme of zero-based budgeting on 1 July 20XX supported by an external facilitator.
2. Complete a review of assessment procedures by 31 December 20XX.	Appoint a consultant with expertise in this area to undertake this review.
3. Investigate and report on the use of handheld recording devices by staff by 28 February 20XX.	Commission a small team of staff led by an Assistant Director to undertake a study.

And by this point . . .

Having read the analysis and direction sections, the reader should now understand the context within which the plan is prepared and the intended direction. However, it is difficult at this point for the reader to be confident about approving the plan as they have a limited under-standing of the actions envisaged, the resource implications and associated risk.

Action planning

The action planning section of the plan should persuade the reader that planned actions have been thought through, are feasible, likely to happen and will be successful.

The following questions are helpful in generating content for this section.

1. How will we ensure that the plan will happen?
2. What resources are needed to support the plan?
3. What risks are plan activities exposed to and how will these be managed?

1. How will we ensure that the plan will happen?

This question can be broken into three detailed questions.

1. What actions are required to make the plan happen and when will these occur?
2. Who is responsible for taking the required actions?
3. How will these actions be monitored?

The answers to these questions can be presented using an Action Plan format as shown in Table 4.16, which is a simple extension of the high level action summary (Table 4.15).

The action plan should contain sufficient detail of planned actions, timings, responsibility and monitoring arrangements for the reader to appreciate the potential impact on the service, staff in general and members of the management team in particular.

Completing the action plan involves:

- inserting the objectives and high level actions in columns 1 and 2 as already identified in the high level actions summary;
- breaking high level actions down into more detailed actions and inserting these in column 3;
- entering key dates for each detailed action in column 4;
- stating in column 5 the name of the person responsible for ensuring that each detailed action occurs. Usually this person will be a member of the management team, although they may delegate this to a member of staff;
- specifying the strategic monitoring arrangements, for example, regular reporting to the management team, supervision, etc., in column 6.

A common problem with plans prepared at higher organisational levels is that too much detail is provided. The Action Plan is not intended to provide the full detail of how objectives are to be pursued; this should be developed as appropriate in other plans such as team plans, project plans, individual workload plans and training plans, etc.

2. What resources are needed to support the plan?

The resources needed to support the plan should be identified during the planning process and a decision made regarding how much detail is included in the plan document. This decision needs to take account of the context, how the plan is to be used and who will have access to it. If the document is only for internal use inclusion of considerable resource detail, perhaps even the full budget, may be appropriate. With external readers, who may not need this level of resource detail, there are normally concerns about confidentiality. In many instances, it is better for the plan to include only broad headline figures and for internal readers to be referred to budget documents for financial information.

Irrespective of where financial detail is included, those preparing plans need to identify:

- the physical resources required to fulfil the plan, for example, beds, staff, equipment;
- the money required to pay for the physical resources which will either be classified as day-to-day running expenses or one-off purchases;
- income from all sources.

This information forms the budget for year one and financial forecasts for years two and three of the plan period.

3. What risks are plan activities exposed to and how will these be managed?

Assuming the organisation already has a robust approach to risk management, and that this has appropriately informed the earlier analysis and direction sections of the document, all that remains is to identify and address new risks associated with proposed actions. The aim here is to assure the reader that new or changed risks have been identified during planning and that these have been considered and will be managed appropriately.

The time spent on risk management and the amount of detail provided should reflect the size, complexity and nature of the service, together with how this is developing. Specialist support may be needed where the level and type of risk is significant. For many plans, however, risk can be addressed by simply completing a grid similar to that included as Table 4.17.

Columns 1, 2 and 3 should be used to identify the source of the risk, describe the risk and explain the likely impact. Columns 4 and 5 should be used to indicate the potential impact and likelihood of occurrence by using a score of 1–10 where 1 is considered low and 10 high. Column 6 should show the impact of combining potential impact and likelihood scores to give a total risk score – the closer this figure is to 100 the more significant the perceived risk. The final column is used to indicate the intended approach to managing this risk.

Summary

Once drafted the plan and the budget should be submitted together for discussion and negotiation, then edited and approved. By the end of this process, potential readers should have a document that is clear, useful and which contains sufficient information to address their particular needs. As this can be quite challenging, it is not unusual for planners to decide to prepare two or more versions of the plan containing different levels of detail, written for different audiences.

Table 4.16 Action plan

Objectives	High level actions	Second level actions	Second level actions – key dates	Responsible person	Monitoring arrangements
(1)	(2)	(3)	(4)	(5)	(6)
To reduce gross revenue spending by 5% in real terms year on year taking the 20XX/XX approved budget as the start point.	Start a rolling programme of zero-based budgeting on 1 July 20XX supported by an external facilitator.	Appoint external facilitator	By 30/4/XX	Ian Charge	Include in monthly performance monitoring process.
		Brief staff	By 31/05/XX		
		Develop programme	By 31/05/XX		
		Start first review	Start 14/6/XX		
Complete a review of assessment procedures by 31 December 20XX	Appoint a consultant with expertise in this area to undertake this review.	Prepare brief	By 31/05/XX	Sue Preemo	Project management procedures and monthly performance monitoring review process.
		Procure consultant	By 31/07/XX		
Investigate and report on the use of handheld reporting devices by staff by 28 February 20XX.	Commission a small team of staff led by an Assistant Director to undertake a study.	Prepare brief	By 31/5/0X	Meg Abite	
		Select staff	By 30/6/0X		

Table 4.17 Risk analysis

Source of risk	Description of risk	Description of likely impact	Impact severity (Score 1–10, where 1 is low and 10 is high)	Likelihood (Score 1–10, where 1 is low and 10 is high)	Risk score (Column 4 x Column 5)	Planned actions
(1)	(2)	(3)	(4)	(5)	(6)	(7)
Objective: to reduce gross revenue spending by 5% in real terms year on year taking the 20XX/XX approved budget as the start point.	Zero-based reviews fall behind schedule due to poor management	Budget will be overspent	8	9	72	Use organisational approved project planning methodology
		Unit costs may be higher than planned				Monthly progress reviews with assistant director
		Service cuts may be imposed				
		Adverse publicity				
		Budget management may be taken back to centre				
	Failure to find 5% cost reduction.	As above	8	6	48	Include external representation to challenge thinking
						Brief team thoroughly, undertake and address training needs analysis

Section 5
Budgeting and financial management

In a general sense, everyone who works for an organisation has some responsibility for, and involvement in, financial management. CIPFA (the Chartered Institute of Public Finance and Accountancy), to which many public sector accountants belong, states in its good practice guide relating to financial regulations (2001: 5) that:

All members and staff have a general responsibility for taking reasonable action to provide for the security of assets under their control, and for ensuring that the use of these resources is legal, is properly authorised, provides value for money and achieves best value.

In addition, many employees are directly involved in financial management through being responsible for a budget or issuing purchase orders, passing invoices for payment, receiving and banking income, etc.

This section introduces financial management, which is part of the wider context within which budget management takes place.

An introduction to financial management

Although many textbooks use the term 'financial management', few authors offer a definition. The contents pages of finance books are evidence that this subject is broad, typically including topics such as:

- financial reporting;
- managing working capital, banking and investments;
- financial control, audit and risk;
- *budget preparation;*
- *budgetary control;*
- acquiring funding;
- cost accounting, short- and long-term decision making;
- performance management;
- project and investment appraisal.

This text concerns just two of the above aspects of financial management; budget preparation and budgetary control, these being ones that managers tend to encounter early on in their career.

Financial management involves the intelligent use of financial tools and processes in support of the organisational vision. Service managers encounter financial tools and processes and, therefore, financial management, when:

- completing plans and exercising managerial control, this including budgeting;
- reporting performance, this including financial measures such as unit costs;
- making decisions, these incorporating cost and other financial information;
- assessing and managing risk to service users, staff, the organisation and society of loss or fraud, this involving financial regulations and procedures;
- reviewing economy, efficiency and effectiveness.

Consistent with the breadth of financial management is a wide range of related competencies needed to run a successful organisation, as possessed by organisational staff and/or external advisors. In rare circumstances one person may possess all the required competences, but, more typically and desirably, these responsibilities and competencies are dispersed throughout the organisation.

Sound financial management relies on a three-way partnership between accountants, administrative staff and managers; each with their own role, yet dependent on the others. Figure 5.1 summarises the typical contribution expected from each party; the overlaps indicating integrated working which, in this example, could be developed further. In practice, the size of each circle and the extent of overlap reflect the approach to financial management found in an organisation.

Decentralised organisations have a relatively large managerial circle and smaller accountant circle, while the opposite is true where a centralised approach is favoured. Irrespective of the adopted approach, the extent of the administrator contribution and, therefore, the size of their circle tends to remain the same. However, *where* administration actually takes place often reflects whether the approach is centralised or decentralised, tending to be at the centre for the former and within departments or service areas with the latter.

Arguably, some aspects of financial management should be undertaken by managers while other aspects are better completed by accountants or administrators. Care needs to be taken to avoid duplication, gaps or an inappropriate sharing of duties, for example, where accountants undertake aspects of budget management that should be part of the manager's role. An inappropriate sharing of duties can arise where a manager fails to engage in budget matters, where organisational leaders expect accountants rather than managers to 'balance the books' and where accountants fear they will be held to account for overspends that lie outside of their control.

Managers need to be competent in those aspects of financial management they personally undertake, while in respect of those aspects of financial management undertaken by accountants, they merely need sufficient understanding to interpret the information they receive, contribute ideas and express views as required.

Although financial management should be an integral part of general management, this is not always the case, particularly in the public sector. Failing to integrate often results in:

- plans that do not reconcile with budgets;
- judgements regarding performance being based largely on budget information;
- crucial strategic decisions being made using incomplete or poor quality information.

Reasons for a lack of integration stem from:

- a tradition in this sector of failing to link cost with activity, although this may be improving as organisations respond to the current economic situation;
- continued pressure to reduce net expenditure with some use made of across-the-board cuts;

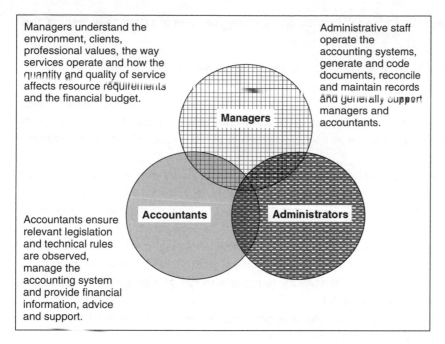

Managers understand the environment, clients, professional values, the way services operate and how the quantity and quality of service affects resource requirements and the financial budget.

Administrative staff operate the accounting systems, generate and code documents, reconcile and maintain records and generally support managers and accountants.

Accountants ensure relevant legislation and technical rules are observed, manage the accounting system and provide financial information, advice and support.

Managers

Accountants

Administrators

Figure 5.1 Key player involvement

- insufficient engagement of managers in financial matters with a consequential over-reliance on accounting staff.

The importance of financial management

There is no 'magic formula' for ensuring effective financial management – organisational leaders have to choose whether to:

- make decisions regarding financial management as and when required; or
- think strategically about financial management.

The former approach leads to dated, ad hoc, inconsistent, ineffective and often contradictory approaches to financial management which in turn can lead to:

- low value for money due to poor resource allocation, monitoring and management;
- financial loss for service users and the organisation;
- relatively low protection for individual staff who may be exposed to false accusations of fraud or poor financial management;
- a lack of evidence that the organisation is managing resources in a safe and wise way;
- poor use of time with organisational leaders increasingly involved in financial trouble-shooting rather than pursuing the purpose of the organisation;
- poor compliance with the principles of good governance and reduced public confidence and support for the organisation;
- finance being seen as technically difficult, shrouded in mystery and, therefore, better undertaken by finance staff. This leads to undue dependency on accountants and managers who become increasingly disengaged and disempowered;

- managerial 'game playing' focused on 'working the system' rather than leading their service.

Over time, decisions made regarding financial management form a framework within which members of the organisation operate. Whatever frameworks are set, managers will engage in practices that minimise adverse affects on their service. These practices, while entirely predictable and understandable, are often not in the best interests of other parts of the organisation, the organisation as a whole or even in the long-term interest of the manager concerned.

Practice regarding financial management is also affected by the quality of information systems and the behaviour of politicians, senior managers and finance staff. Budget managers can be expected to engage in 'game playing' to protect or promote their service, even where this adversely affects other services or, for example, future generations. Organisational leaders are responsible for developing an approach to financial management that minimises the likelihood of unhelpful or inappropriate managerial practice. Table 5.1 provides examples of poor frameworks, systems and behaviours, together with typical managerial responses that, while understandable, are unhelpful.

To avoid these and other unhelpful behaviours, leaders of organisations should pay attention to determining how financial management will occur in the future, ensuring that this is consistent with the overall recipe for organisational success.

Main elements and evolution

Good financial management requires appropriate frameworks, effective systems, competent staff and appropriate behaviour from all those involved, as shown in Figure 5.2.

The frameworks, systems, competent staff and behaviours of those involved in financial management need to be consistent with both the purpose and culture of the organisation. Furthermore, the overall approach to financial management needs to flex quickly in response to environment changes.

Table 5.1 Typical responses to poor frameworks, systems and behaviours

Poor frameworks, systems and behaviours	Typical managerial responses
A common rule that money unspent at the end of the year is taken away from the budget manager and future budgets reduced accordingly.	Budget managers ensure they do not have unspent money by engaging in a 'spending spree' in March.
Budgets that appear to be underspending during the year are 'raided' by line managers and the proceeds given to overspending managers.	Budget managers ensure spending is high early in the year, may overstate commitments, massage estimates of the year end financial position, etc.
Draft budgets are cut by 5% to encourage economy and efficiency.	Managers ask for more budget than they need, knowing they will get less than they ask for.

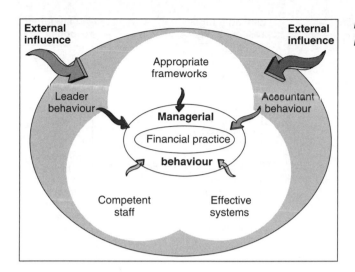

Figure 5.2 Financial management – overview

Appropriate frameworks

While leaders of organisations have significant freedom to determine the approach to financial management, they need to recognise:

- external factors such as legislation, regulation, accounting convention and funding agency requirements;
- internal factors including the values and preferences of politicians, senior officers and accountants.

In practice, organisations use a number of frameworks to determine how managers will undertake budget management. The financial structure, the budgets assigned to managers, roles and responsibilities, financial regulations, procedure notes and plans, are examples of such frameworks, and are explored below.

Structure and scope of responsibility

Organisations tend to be divided into departments, services, establishments, etc., each of which are the responsibility of a manager who will plan and control activity. Typically, these managers also have a degree of financial responsibility, the nature of which can vary significantly within and between organisations. Information about costs will be recorded in a way that can be traced to these areas of responsibility, often referred to as cost centres, defined by Drury (1994: 32) as being 'where managers are accountable for the expenses under their control'.

Organisational leaders have considerable freedom regarding the cost centre structure and the associated range of budgets. The scope of budget responsibility ranges from managing a limited number of budgets, typically those over which the manager can exercise some degree of control, to full budget responsibility where managers manage budgets that cover the cost of all the physical resources they use, irrespective of whether they can exercise direct control. Figure 5.3 illustrates both limited and full responsibility situations.

Ultimately, the scope of budget responsibility is determined by politicians and senior managers who vary in their willingness to relinquish the associated power.

Figure 5.3 Extent of responsibility

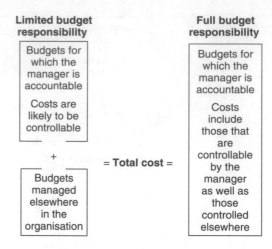

ACTIVITY 5.1

Controllable expenditure

The following table identifies four budgets relating to a day centre for older people.

To what extent do you think the manager might be able to control expenditure?

Budget	Not able to control	Limited control	Good level of control	Full control
Rent				
Heat and light				
Food				
Equipment				

For many managers, rent costs are totally outside their control, at least in the short term, while the level of control they have over other costs will depend on the framework within which they are required to manage.

Taking equipment as an example, financial regulations might be set so as to allow full managerial control, partial managerial control or to make this expenditure virtually uncontrollable by the budget manager.

Figure 5.4 illustrates how financial regulations might be set in a way that severely limits managerial control over an equipment budget.

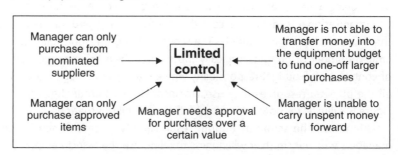

Figure 5.4 Control factors – equipment

ACTIVITY *5.2*

Increasing the level of local control

- *Identify three budgets from within your cost centre and describe the extent to which these are controllable*
- *What changes would need to be made to financial regulations or other frameworks to increase the level of local control?*

Managers of cost centres are usually required to meet a simple financial target – to keep within budget. Those with more extensive responsibility may find they are also required to keep within a target unit cost.

While many social care and health managers are responsible for a cost centre, a few are actually responsible for a profit centre, defined by Drury (1994: 32) as being 'where managers are accountable for sales revenue and expenses; for example, a division of a company that is responsible for the selling and production of a product'. While profit centres are more commonly found in the private sector, this type of responsibility can be found in the public and voluntary sectors, for example, where the public are charged a fee for a service or where one part of an organisation 'sells' a service to other parts, e.g. a design and print unit.

Although referred to as 'profit centres', in practice, within the public and voluntary sector the financial target is often to balance income and expenditure or even to keep within a target loss. The definition of what constitutes a profit centre does not, therefore, depend on the intended or actual financial outcome, nor is it simply to do with having responsibility for income; indeed many cost centres have minor sources of income, for example, from charging staff for making private telephone calls.

Profit centres tend to share a number of characteristics:

- income is usually a significant element in financing the service;
- income is not guaranteed or predictable and has to be 'earned' from customers, purchasers or grant givers;
- a failure to generate budgeted income might well lead to the cessation of the profit centre;
- the manager finds themselves worrying about the volume of work and prices they charge as much as (if not more than) they do about expenditure;
- business planning rather than service planning is used;
- depending on the financial regulations of the organisation, the manager might be allowed to carry any surplus funds over at the end of the year or set a deficit against earlier surpluses;
- performance reporting tends to be similar to that found in the private sector;
- overall 'bottom line' financial targets are likely to be set in terms of surplus, deficit or break even.

Roles and responsibilities

A clear allocation of financial roles and responsibilities is crucial to effective financial management. These roles include budget management, income collection and recovery, petty cash management, order processing, inventory management and stock control.

49

Financial responsibilities should be included in job descriptions and the organisation should maintain a register that shows for each budget the name of the manager responsible. Each budget manager should:

- be aware of the financial responsibilities related to their job;
- understand how their financial performance will be measured;
- know the regulations relevant to their responsibilities;
- possess the competencies associated with the effective discharge of their role.

And they should know the size of their budget before the year begins.

Financial regulations and procedure notes

Financial regulations specify what managers must and must not do, and procedure notes set out how to comply with these regulations in a consistent, efficient and effective way.

Financial regulations and procedure notes form a vital part of internal control and compliance with these should be routinely checked to reduce the risk of financial loss, fraud, inefficiency and harm to staff or service users.

ACTIVITY **5·3**

Financial regulations – understanding

Find the financial regulations of your organisation and any associated procedure notes.*

- *With reference to your job description and current work responsibilities, read those parts of the financial regulations and associated procedures that apply to you.*
- *Make a note of any areas that you are not clear about, ask the relevant person for clarification and record the outcome.*

Plans

Financial management should be an integral part of service management. As explored earlier, plans are the means by which direction and intent are described and the budget is simply the financial expression of the cost of acquiring the use of the physical resources needed. The plan, therefore, becomes a vital framework for budget management in particular and financial management in general.

Unfortunately, in practice plans and budgets are often poorly linked which makes performance management difficult and leaves the manager particularly vulnerable to pressure to:

- cut planned expenditure while maintaining service volume and quality;
- increase service volume and/or quality but within existing budget levels;
- cut expenditure levels while increasing service volume and/or quality.

Repeated yielding to any of these pressures should be impossible, for this implies that it is possible to have an infinite volume of service at maximum quality without requiring resources

---

* While most organisations have financial regulations or the equivalent, fewer have written procedure notes, at least not within a single definitive document.

or budget – a neat trick. Even if, in the early years of financial constraint, savings can be made without adversely affecting the service, a point will be reached after which further savings can only be achieved by:

- reducing service quality, probably aspects that are not reflected in service standards or performance indicators;
- staff 'volunteering' to work in excess of contracted hours and without pay – in effect, offering a hidden personal subsidy arising from a personal commitment to service users, fears regarding job security, or in the mistaken belief that this is only a short-term necessity;
- passing expenses to the next generation of taxpayers, for example, by allowing buildings, equipment and other resources to quietly deteriorate.

If plans and budgets are integrated, any reduction in allocated resources will need to be balanced by a reduction in the quantity and/or quality of planned activity – an honest and transparent approach.

Effective systems

Effective financial management requires good quality financial and service information.

The principle source of financial information is usually the main accounting system, which is operated by finance staff and through which vast numbers of transactions pass each year. However sophisticated this system may be, it is unlikely to satisfy all the financial information needs of managers who inevitably maintain some local systems, for example, in respect of official orders for which invoices have not been paid, grant claims, bid information or unit cost data.

Increasingly, public service managers need information that requires finance and service data to be combined as is the case, for example, with unit costs. This is quite a challenge, particularly as separate systems still exist in many organisations.

Good quality financial information requires well-designed and correctly operated systems accompanied by regulations, procedure notes and compliance monitoring that helps ensure these remain effective.

ACTIVITY **5.4**

Financial regulations – checking

What arrangements exist within your service for checking that staff comply with financial regulations?

Competent staff

Successful financial management requires that everyone involved is competent, which in turn necessitates the regular review and addressing of individual development needs associated with understanding financial frameworks, and using systems, processes and financial techniques.

Unfortunately, in many organisations training expenditure devoted to developing financial competence is often allocated to meeting the needs of managers and accountants rather than administrators. The lack of training for administrative staff can lead to inconsistent practices across an organisation.

Financial management is far from just a collection of processes or techniques. Success depends on accountants, administrators and managers understanding and valuing each other and being able to collaborate to provide good quality financial and management information. Competence and mutual trust regarding competence is essential.

Financial leadership

While much is written about financial management, little reference is made to financial leadership other than in respect to finance staff. As with other aspects of organisational life, a distinction can be drawn between what is done (management) and how it is done (leadership). It is possible for an organisation to have excellent arrangements regarding financial practice; budgets are prepared and controlled, income collected promptly and decisions incorporate financial information. The management, or 'what', of finance is fine; however, the way this is done might not lead to high levels of performance. For example, a line manager who emphasises control, acts coercively and applies sanctions is likely to find their budget managers perform less well than one who coaches their staff.

Financial leadership, which can be defined as thoughtful engagement in the how of financial management, occurs where:

- the approach to finance is consciously considered as part of the overall culture;
- the budget process is seen as a learning opportunity as well as a means of control;
- the contributions of those with financial roles and responsibilities are clearly linked to service vision;
- those with financial responsibility are empowered, encouraged and coached;
- rational budgeting and creative use of resources are encouraged;
- decisions and actions involving finance are informed by shared values.

In financially difficult times, organisations typically centralise control, impose sweeping bans (for example, on filling staff vacancies) and introduce tight spending approval processes. Irrespective of whether these actions are appropriate, the way they are introduced will affect motivation, behaviour and performance. Poor financial leadership will simply lead to increased game playing.

Section 6
The budget manager role

This section examines the role of budget manager by reference to the degree of decentralisation within the organisation and whether budgets are devolved or delegated. The nature of responsibilities and rights is also explored, as are the associated financial competences.

Decentralisation, devolution and delegation

While the budgets of a very small organisation may be managed effectively by one person, this approach is not normally possible, or appropriate, for larger and more complex organisations; a degree of decentralisation is usually required, defined by Bean and Hussey (1996: 6) as being:

Where the control of budgets is disaggregated from the centre and allocated to other areas of the organisation such as departments, divisions, branches etc.

Organisational leaders determine both the extent of decentralisation within the organisation and the nature of managerial responsibility, this normally being either devolved or delegated in nature.

Devolved budget management is defined by Bean and Hussey (1996: 5) as:

The process whereby budgets are devolved to an individual who becomes the budget holder and who will be totally responsible and accountable for that budget. Ideally, management and financial responsibilities are aligned such that the budget holder is accountable for the financial implications of his/her management decisions.

The term 'totally responsible' is important and needs qualification. The devolved budget holder is responsible for taking action that is within their authority including alerting their line manager to problems they cannot control as soon as possible.

The delegated approach is defined by Bean and Hussey (1996: 6) as being:

Where budgets are delegated to nominated budget holders who are responsible for monitoring the budget, but are not accountable for the budget as they will have little or no control over its construction and its usage.

By comparison with devolved budgeting, delegated responsibility is limited with the budget holder simply required to:

- spend an allocated budget on agreed types of purchase, broadly in line with an anticipated pattern of expenditure throughout the year;

- regularly monitor the budget, investigate and report problems to the person who actually holds devolved responsibility.

In larger organisations, there may be considerable decentralisation of budgets some of which are devolved, others delegated.

Although both the devolved and delegated approaches are valid and can be effective, until recently devolution was more fashionable. However, a classic response to recession is to centralise responsibility and spending control so devolution is currently being reversed in many public service organisations.

It is quite common to find organisations that claim to have devolved budgets when, in practice, the approach is a confused and ineffective combination of devolution and delegation; a form of pseudo-devolution.

Figure 6.1 summarises the main differences between devolved and delegated approaches to budget management and compares these with the pseudo-devolved approach.

For the devolved budget manager, the budget represents a financial target which, as with other targets, they should understand and believe to be fair, yet challenging. A reasonable expectation, therefore, is that a devolved budget manager will have adequate opportunities to be involved in budget preparation, negotiation and control.

Having a reasonable degree of freedom to act, for example, the ability to move money from one budget to another, or exercise choice as to where purchases are made, is also important to managers with devolved responsibility.

Involvement in budget preparation and negotiation is much less important to the delegated budget manager. As their responsibility is less onerous it is acceptable for a delegated budget manager to be given a budget together with guidance regarding the purpose for which this is to be used. The main task of the delegated budget holder is to periodically examine the budget position, investigate problems as they arise and alert their line manager to underspends or overspends that exceed a certain size. Subsequent action in response to the budget position rests with the manager who has delegated this responsibility.

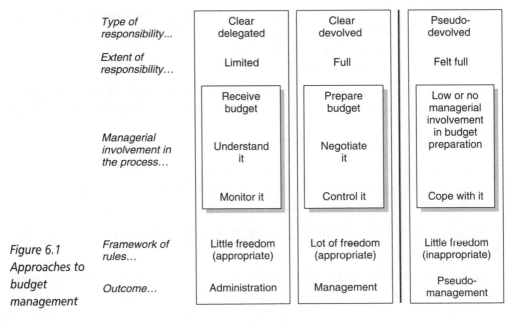

	Clear delegated	Clear devolved	Pseudo-devolved
Type of responsibility...	Clear delegated	Clear devolved	Pseudo-devolved
Extent of responsibility...	Limited	Full	Felt full
Managerial involvement in the process...	Receive budget Understand it Monitor it	Prepare budget Negotiate it Control it	Low or no managerial involvement in budget preparation Cope with it
Framework of rules...	Little freedom (appropriate)	Lot of freedom (appropriate)	Little freedom (inappropriate)
Outcome...	Administration	Management	Pseudo-management

Figure 6.1 Approaches to budget management

Limited freedom to act is appropriate to delegated responsibility as, in effect, the manager is only administering the budget.

With pseudo-devolution, the manager is made to feel fully responsible for achieving the budget while at the same time is denied involvement in preparation. The manager is left unaware of the assumptions underlying the budget and suspicious that it may be insufficient to resource the plan. This problem is compounded where the budget manager has little freedom to react to emerging budget underspends or overspends. Whereas budget devolution causes power to shift down the organisation, with pseudo-devolution it is stress, rather than power, that is devolved.

Financial responsibilities

For many managers, budget management is their main, but not necessarily their only, financial responsibility. Managers in different service areas, and at different managerial levels, may have quite varied financial responsibilities, the full extent of which should be clear from their job description.

Effective budget management is dependent on politicians, leaders and accountants acknowledging and responding to the rights of the budget manager, the number and nature of which varies according to whether responsibility is devolved or delegated.

Table 6.1 suggests some of the responsibilities and rights relevant to a devolved budget manager operating at a relatively low organisational level. It should be noted that the 'rights' associated with budget management are not widely recognised, at least formally, within organisations.

The approach to financial management should be regularly reviewed to ensure it supports the intended culture of the organisation. This review should also consider the responsibilities and rights of budget managers.

ACTIVITY **6.1**

Financial responsibility

In respect of your service area, identify the budget manager and carry out the following tasks.

- *Establish whether they have devolved, delegated, or pseudo-devolved responsibility.*
- *Identify their formal responsibilities with regard to budget management.*
- *Establish or propose a set of rights appropriate to their responsibilities.*
- *Reach a view as to whether their rights are observed by the organisation.*

Financial competencies – managers

The breadth of financial competence needed by managers depends on the approach to finance within the organisation, their managerial level, whether budget responsibility is devolved or delegated and the level of support received from accountants and administrative staff.

Depending on their responsibilities, devolved budget managers should be able to:

- prepare a budget;
- monitor a budget;

Table 6.1 Responsibilities and rights

Financial responsibilities **You are responsible for:**	Financial rights **You have the right to:**
Reading and ensuring you understand and keep up to date with financial regulations and procedures.	Know if you are a budget holder and to be aware of the quantity and quality of service to be achieved with the approved budget.
Participating fully in budget preparation.	Know the nature of your financial responsibility and the performance targets that apply.
Undertaking monthly budget monitoring and year end projecting, taking action as required to keep within the approved budget.	Be properly involved in preparing, negotiating and agreeing a challenging, yet achievable, budget.
Alerting senior managers and finance staff at the earliest opportunity to actual or projected budget under/over spends, fraud, etc.	Know the amount of your budget before the financial year starts.
Ensuring that relevant information informs plans, funding bids, performance management and decisions.	Be consulted before any changes are made to the agreed budget during the year.
Discharging other financial duties in a timely and professional manner, e.g. making grant claims and invoice raising.	Receive advance notice of planned charges to your budget and have the opportunity to check, challenge and agree to these.
Monitoring observance of financial regulations and processes.	Be informed of the financial regulations and procedures within which you are required to work.
Pursuing value for money.	Receive relevant, clear, accurate and timely budget information and advice.
	An appropriate level of training and development prior to assuming financial responsibility.

- prepare year end forecasts taking effective action including, as necessary, escalating budget issues within the organisation.

Delegated budget managers need to be able to monitor a budget, investigate variances and suggest possible control action.

In addition, all budget managers should understand:

- the role, responsibilities and rights associated with their post;
- the financial regulations and procedures within which they are expected to work;
- the budget reporting process and budget reports;
- the political and behavioural aspects of budgeting.

Budget managers should periodically review their competence in the light of anticipated changes in the external environment and their likely future responsibilities. This latter point encourages a manager to start preparing for their next financial role, which will often be more strategic, broad and complex.

At a more strategic level, effective management may involve the use of specialist financial techniques and require a deeper understanding of financial management. Reassuringly perhaps, senior managers do not need to train to become accountants; as their roles become more onerous the level of technical support received from finance specialists should increase. It is important, however, that the manager:

- resists the temptation to transfer their responsibility for finance to accounting staff;
- has a broad understanding of financial techniques, can participate in their use and sensitively interpret and act upon the outcomes.

Section 7

Budget management – preparation

This section defines budget management, provides an overview of the main processes involved and outlines the different ways in which budgets can be prepared.

Definitions

For the purpose of this text, budget management is:

The total process by which budgets are prepared, negotiated, monitored and acted upon.

An expenditure budget is defined as:

The estimated cost of acquiring the use of the physical resources needed to pursue the actions planned to achieve the objectives, and ultimately the mission of the organisation.

And an income budget is defined as:

The estimated fees, charges, grants or other funding associated with the provision of one or more services, or activities.

Two aspects of the above definitions are important. Firstly, budgets reflect a chosen view of the future and it follows, therefore, that to some extent they will probably be incorrect. Secondly, there is an assumed link between the budget and the plan.

While budgets can be expressed in units of physical resource (e.g. staff hours, miles, etc.) they are more commonly expressed in financial terms and fall into two main types; those concerned with day to day running expenses and income (revenue), and others with the purchase of items broadly expected to last more than one year (capital).

Figure 7.1 illustrates how, in practice, planning and budgeting are often managed as two separate processes, with the attendant risk that these produce different and unreconciled views of the future.

A charitable view is that poor linkage results from the difficulty that managers in the service sector have in identifying how much physical resource is required for a certain level and quality of service. An alternative view is that if the linkage is denied or unclear, senior managers, politicians and society are free to demand increasingly higher levels and standards of service while maintaining or reducing resources.

As argued previously, plans and budgets should be integrated, with both appearing as a single document or alternatively as two documents that dovetail. Figure 7.2 shows the integrated process in which physical resources clearly feature. By comparison, physical resources

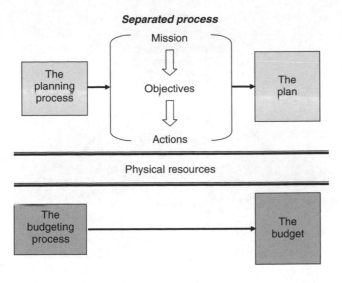

Figure 7.1 Separated process

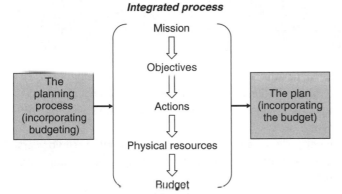

Figure 7.2 Integrated process

tend not to be taken into account in either the plan or budget where separation is the practice. Knowledge of the quantity and quality of physical resources needed to fulfil a plan and to calculate the budget is the key to integration.

Budget management involves two major processes; preparation and control as shown in Figure 7.3, which also shows that these link with activity management which incorporates planning.

Budget preparation involves calculating, negotiating, revising and agreeing the budget. Budgetary control involves checking, investigating, projecting and acting. The two processes of preparation and control should be managed so as to maximise learning; sound preparation should lead to learning that will assist with future budgetary control and sound control should inform preparation of the next budget.

An effective approach to budget management will:

- stimulate and improve service planning, coordination and control across the organisation;
- help ensure that plans are honest and realistic given the level of available resource, thereby minimising the risk that quality will be eroded;
- encourage the discussion of service priorities.

59

Figure 7.3 Budget management in context

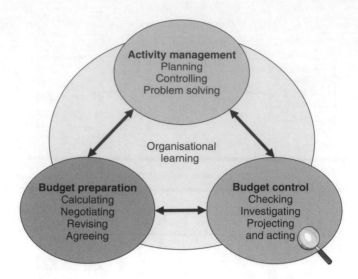

Unfortunately, the practice of budget management is often poor and organisations fail to realise these potential benefits.

The budget cycle

Organisations tend to engage in similar patterns of budget management activity during the year, due in part to many of them working to the same financial year, which runs from April to March. However, the precise timings of the stages involved vary to reflect the size, complexity and approach to budget management.

In larger organisations, the budget cycle for a particular year may spread over two years, starting nine or more months before the year in question and concluding approximately three months after, as indicated in Figure 7.4.

Budget and planning cycles should be similar and linked, both being preceded by high-level discussions regarding the likely future environment as informed by a corporate SPELT analysis. This will include factors such as anticipated pay settlements, inflation rates, interest rates, government grants and the financial implications of new legislation. The information derived from SPELT allows those planning to reach an initial view of 'how next year might look' in terms of likely overall resource levels and budget pressures. Once this future view is known, detailed plan and budget preparation commences and a cycle of preparation, negotiation and revision is repeated several times as key factors (e.g. grant settlements and likely inflation) become clearer, closer to the start of the budget year. Budgets and service plans, therefore, often need to be fine-tuned prior to formal corporate agreement or approval.

Final plan and budget approval occur almost immediately before the budget year starts and the manager's attention then turns to performance monitoring, including budgetary control. Budgetary control, which is normally undertaken on a monthly basis, involves assessing and responding to the financial position to date and as anticipated for the year end.

Towards the end of the budget year, and continuing into the early part of the next year, attention shifts to closing the accounts, a process that ensures all income and expenditure relating to the budget year is identified and coded to the correct budgets. Closure, which is largely a technical exercise, tends to involve finance staff and administrators more than managers and results in the preparation of the final set of accounts.

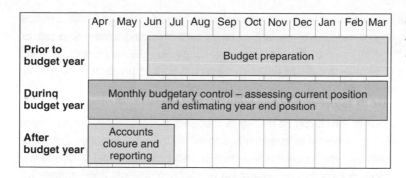

Figure 7.4
A typical
budget cycle

In recent years, two changes to the traditional budget cycle have occurred; firstly, local authorities have been required to close accounts more quickly so the whole cycle ends earlier than it used to. Secondly, the preparation process tends to start earlier due to pressure on resources and greater complexity associated with increased partnership working. In some organisations the planning process is now continual, with regular environmental scanning and modelling of financial impact, particularly at a corporate level.

Multi-agency working, which frequently involves resource sharing, means those engaged in planning need to time the multi-agency planning and budget preparation process so that it fits the cycles of different agencies. Failure to coordinate can leave a multi-agency team submitting a resource request for next year that is too late to be considered in the current round of agency plans and budgets.

Budget preparation

When preparing budgets an important aim is to ensure that planned activity can be resourced. As managers are rarely happy to reduce the quantity or quality of services they manage there is a risk that they may accept, or even propose, a budget that is insufficient for planned activity, preferring to hope it will all 'work out' rather than confront the potential need for service reductions. While occasionally luck, or improvements in operational efficiency, enable a plan to be achieved with less resource than originally estimated, it is more likely that a failure to confront a budget shortfall will lead to:

- overspent budgets at the year end;
- lower actual than planned volumes of service which allows the manager to keep within budget but which results in higher than budgeted unit costs;
- a fall in the quality of the service which will probably be evident to service users but not necessarily noticed or acknowledged within the organisation;
- action that will have a negative long-term impact, for example, failure to adequately maintain buildings or to develop staff;
- further increased pressure on staff which, in the longer term, may have cost implications.

There is a need for senior managers, political leaders and society to own the relationship between planned service provision, resource consumption and cost. If there is a wish to devote less money to a particular service the outcome of this needs to be recognised and owned at all organisational levels – pretending that the level of quantity and quality of service can be forever maintained while the level of resource is reduced year on year is unsustainable.

The first of the four stages involved in budget preparation is calculation, which usually involves finance staff preparing an initial version of the budget based on the existing budget adjusted, or not, for the effects of inflation and other cost pressures between the two years. In those organisations that fail to engage devolved budget managers in budget preparation, or where these managers lack competence or confidence, there is a danger that this initial version of the budget is simply accepted, perhaps in the belief that as it was prepared by an accountant, it will be reliable. It is essential that devolved budget managers check any budget figures given to them to see if they look reasonable, either by independently calculating the resources they think they need or, at least, by reference to their experience of historic and current budget performance. While delegated managers do not need to be engaged in preparation, it is still good practice for them to be consulted as it builds their understanding of the assumptions underpinning the budget and helps prepare them for more demanding responsibilities later in their career.

Budgets are financial targets and should be challenging yet realistic; qualities achieved through rigorous negotiation between the budget manager, their line manager and, ultimately, other stakeholders such as politicians and trustees, etc. To be effective in negotiation, the budget manager needs knowledge of the service, planned activity and the relationship this has with physical resources.

Either the plan and/or the budget may need revision as a result of negotiation, concluding with agreement as to the level of funding which should now be sufficient to resource the planned service.

TIPS FOR SUCCESS

In order to be successful in budget preparation:

- *Managers should be properly engaged and able to reach a view as to the adequacy of the budget.*
- *Sufficient time should be allocated to the budget process.*
- *There needs to be integration with the planning process which should be timed so as to coordinate effort and allow for detailed work.*
- *Managers should have an opportunity to negotiate.*
- *The negotiation stage should be challenging.*
- *Any decision to reduce or cap a budget should be accompanied by those involved owning the resultant implications for the service.*
- *As a result of discussion, budget revision should occur and the budget manager notified of the approved amount.*

As a consequence of poor preparation, budget managers are often unsure of the basis upon which the budget is prepared and are unaware of whether the amount is adequate. This can lead to:

- a lack of commitment to stay within the approved budget amount;
- stress and fear;
- managers being unduly prudent and restricting spending early in the year to be on the 'safe side'. The resultant underspending, which may have been gained as a result of restricting

service provision, is then corrected with a year end 'spend up' which often represents poor value for money;
* poor behaviour, game playing and low morale.

Budget calculating

There are two broad approaches to preparing a budget; rational and historic.

Rational approaches attempt to relate financial budgets to physical resource requirements which, in turn, reflect the volume and quality of planned service. Rational approaches include plan-led, policy-based budgeting, thematic, needs-led and zero-based, etc.

While a good case can be made for rational budgeting, this is a time-consuming process that is likely to yield little benefit if done each year, particularly in respect of services that are relatively stable.

With historic, or incremental budgeting as it is often known, a future budget is based on previous actual figures or, more likely, the existing budget.

In practice, most organisations use a mixture of rational and historic techniques, skewed towards the historic. While rational budgeting may be used for new services or as part of a fundamental review, historic budgeting will tend to be used elsewhere.

Most organisations would benefit from increasing the proportion of budgets prepared on a rational basis, adopting a rolling programme whereby all budgets are completed on this basis one year in three, with a historic approach used for the other two years. Arguably, the current economic environment and associated large budget reductions demand greater use of rational approaches.

Irrespective of whether a rational or historic approach is adopted, all budgets comprise two elements:

* the volume of physical resource to be purchased (e.g. the number of staff to be employed); and
* the price (e.g. annual salary plus employer's national insurance and pension contributions).

These two elements are evident where rational budgeting is used but the process of historic budgeting obscures this, particularly where this simply involves adding an inflation factor to a previous budget figure.

Rational budgeting

The financial calculations associated with rational approaches to budget preparation are typically straightforward. However, estimating the quantity of physical resources required, on which the financial budget is based, can be difficult and requires considerable professional and service knowledge.

There are a number of different forms of rational budgeting including plan-led and zero-based, which are outlined below.

Plan-led budgeting

The case for integrating planning and budgeting processes has been made earlier, the link between these being an estimate of the volume of physical resources required to deliver the plan.

As the most important factor in budget preparation within voluntary and public sector organisations is usually the overall level of available resource, it is sensible to get an early indication of the overall budget situation. This indication, which allows those planning and budgeting to be realistic about their aspirations and, therefore, their plans, should result from a high level environmental scan and be communicated early in the planning cycle.

Zero-based budgeting

In mature organisations it is common to find budgets that have been prepared on a historic basis for many years. The link between the plan and budget is vague at best; the budget is unlikely to have been challenged for some time and may be insufficient, too generous, or even unnecessary.

Zero-based budgeting involves calculating the budget by reference to what is needed rather than previous or existing budget levels. Maximum benefit is derived when long-held assumptions about the need for, quality of and means of delivering the service are challenged. Potentially, zero-based budgeting is a creative process involving deep consideration of what is to be done, how and to what standard. If undertaken well the manager will find the analysis focuses on service activity much more than financial costs and benefits, to the extent that it might be better referred to as zero-based planning.

Those involved in zero-based budgeting should be prepared to:

- challenge commonly held views regarding clients and their needs, the service and professional practice;
- develop a deep understanding of service outcomes and how these might be achieved;
- innovate in terms of service design and delivery.

It should be noted that writers often talk of this process involving 'justification', which is correct in the sense that whatever comes out of the process can be justified. However, in using this term there is a risk of implying that the aim is to justify what exists rather than challenging the status quo; the former being a natural temptation for managers and perhaps reinforced where zero-based budgeting is inappropriately talked of as a cost cutting tool, which severely limits its effectiveness. Stakeholders, anxious to protect budgets, are likely to adopt change resistant postures based on justifying why this budget cannot be reduced rather than considering the value of the service, whether it should continue, and how. If undertaken thoroughly, zero-based budgeting will, on occasion, lead to a case being made for a larger rather than smaller budget, much in the same way as with effective best value studies. Table 7.1 identifies some of the reasons why lower and higher budgets may result from zero-based budgeting.

Challenging questions are at the heart of zero-based budgeting, the phrasing of which reflects the budget under review. Example questions such as those included in Table 7.2 indicate the level of challenge applicable to a budget for travel associated with visiting clients in their own homes in order to undertake an assessment. The questions in this example form an early stage in preparing a zero-based budget, after which an estimate can be made of how many miles will need to be travelled which, when multiplied by the appropriate mileage rate, will lead to a financial budget. Typical of the early stages of zero-based budgeting, the answers to almost all questions involve knowledge of care, standards, professional practice, managerial factors, and so on. In this example, even more radical questions may be possible going beyond issues associated purely with travel and assessment.

Table 7.1 Reasons for lower and higher budgets arising from zero-based budgeting

Lower budgets may result from	Higher budgets may result from
Improved purchasing arrangements leading to economy gains.	A need to correct problems arising from years of pushing costs into the future.
More efficient use of resources resulting in less volume needing to be purchased.	The process revealing practices or standards that are illegal or unacceptable – additional resources may be required to remedy this situation.
Changing delivery processes which may affect the type, volume and mix of resources required. Overall the value of the resources required may fall.	Recognising that a service which might be economic and efficient is not actually meeting the needs of clients and, therefore, of low value – additional resources are required.
A reduction in planned service volumes – therefore, less resource required.	An increase in planned service volume or quality – therefore, more physical resources required.

Table 7.2 Example zero-based budgeting questions

1. What is the reason for visiting the client?
2. Are assessments necessary?
3. Why is it necessary to visit the client in their own home?
4. Why not request that the client visits us or contacts us by telephone?
5. How often should each client be visited?
6. Could the assessment be undertaken as part of any other visit?

If a visit to the client at home is necessary

7. By what means should staff travel?

If, for example, cars are deemed necessary

8. How might journeys be planned in the most travel efficient way?
9. Which is the most cost effective way of organising car travel (e.g. pool cars, company cars, use of private cars)?

If private cars are to be used

10. What is the most appropriate rate to reimburse at?

The advantages and limitations of rational budgeting approaches vary with the actual approach used. Table 7.3 shows these in respect of zero-based budgeting.

It should be noted that many of the limitations associated with zero-based budgeting are reduced if this is undertaken as a rolling programme where a few budgets are subjected to this approach each year.

Historic budgeting

With historic budgeting, the budget for next year is based on previous actual expenditure or, more frequently, the budget relating to the current year.

Table 7.3 Zero-based budgeting – advantages and limitations

Zero-based budgeting	
Advantages are that it...	**Limitations are that it...**
Involves challenging the current service.	Is time consuming and can become unworkable.
Is potentially creative.	Requires an ability and willingness to challenge at all organisational levels.
Engages managers and service professionals in budgeting.	Places additional demands on finance staff.
Is likely to ensure recognition of the service user viewpoint.	Demands considerable non-financial information.
Is a source of organisational learning and demonstrates a commitment to value for money.	Can lead to an outcome that may conflict with the preferences of key stakeholders.

In practice there are two forms of historic budgeting; full and partial. With the former version a fair attempt is made to ensure that the budget for next year adequately takes account of all financial implications of known or anticipated changes in the environment, the service offered or the price of resources required. Table 7.4 is an example of how full incremental budgeting might look in respect of an establishment.

Table 7.4 Historic budgeting – example

Establishment A	£
Budget for 2012/13 (current year)	**1,450,000**
Anticipated service changes (2013/14)	
Reduction in expected occupancy	–30,000
New quality standards	40,000
Implementation of new pay structure	20,000
Staff restructuring	–25,000
	1,455,000
Inflation (Estimated at 3% and rounded up)	44,000
Budget for 2013/14	**1,499,000**

In this example the budgeted figure for 2013/14 (£1,499,000) should be sufficient providing that:

- the current budget for 2012/13 (£1,450,000) adequately reflects planned activity for 2012/13; and
- all changes to service provision and operation in 2013/14 have been anticipated and the estimated financial implications are reasonably accurate.

The advantages and limitations associated with historic budgeting are summarised in Table 7.5.

Table 7.5 Historic budgeting – advantages and limitations

Historic budgeting

Advantages are that it . . .	Limitations are that it . . .
Is easy to undertake and relatively inexpensive, particularly in centralised organisations.	Encourages the separation of planning and budgeting thereby breaking the link between activity and resources.
Is relatively quick to complete so budget preparation can start later in the year.	Encourages the perpetuation of existing services and ways of operating
Results in relatively stable patterns of funding and service provision which assists central control.	Does not normally lead to any slack in the budget being identified.
Is less likely to result in resource rivalry due to increases or decreases tending to be applied incrementally and experienced to a similar extent by different services.	Causes budget preparation to become a technical financial process from which many managers withdraw leading to disempowerment.

Incremental budgeting is widely practiced in a 'partial' form where changes to the budget are made for a limited range of reasons, for example, inflation. This partial, and rather crude, approach has developed due to:

- a general unwillingness to confront resource implications associated with increasing demand for service and improved quality;
- constant pressure to limit public spending;
- a belief that efficiency can be encouraged by setting budgets that are lower than required;
- limited understanding of the link between plans and budgets with consequently little way of knowing if existing budgets are too tight or generous.

Price bases

Irrespective of whether the chosen approach to budgeting is rational or historic, those leading organisations have to decide how to respond to inflation or changing prices.

As budgets are prepared prior to the year to which they relate, the actual price that will be paid for resources is unknown. By the time resources are purchased the price may well be different, usually higher, as can be seen in the following example.

> **EXAMPLE**
>
> *A budget is prepared in November for printer cartridges, to be purchased in the financial year starting next April. Assuming it is expected that 100 printer cartridges will be needed next year and that at the date the budget is prepared these cost £20 each. Based on this price the budget needed next year will be £2,000 (100 times £20). This budget will prove sufficient if*

> *the planned volume (100 cartridges) is purchased and the price applying throughout next year remains at £20. However, if the price were to rise to £21 from 1 April and remain at this level for the whole year the cost of 100 cartridges would be £2,100, which exceeds the original budget. Assuming the manager decides to keep within the budget by reducing the number of cartridges, only 95 can be purchased (£2,000/21).*

Inflation can be a significant problem, particularly when the rate is high and/or volatile; the risk being that the money available in the year will be insufficient to purchase the level of goods and services required to deliver the plan.

Leaders of organisations have two main options for dealing with inflation.

1. Option A – Base the budget on the price that applied at the date budget preparation takes place. Many years ago this was a common way of pricing a budget and works providing the budget manager is given additional money during the year if actual prices rise. However, while this approach protects the service provider from inflation it causes problems for those providing funding as they cannot entirely predict how much they will have to give to the service provider.

2. Option B – Base the budget on prices that it is expected will be paid during the year to which the budget relates, by incorporating an allowance for future inflation. Normally with this basis, once the budget is agreed it remains fixed during the year irrespective of whether the amount of inflation was estimated correctly. This approach works well for budget managers providing that future inflation is estimated correctly and is helpful to service funders who will know with certainty how much they will pay for a service.

Returning to the last example, the following figures compare the two approaches to inflation:

If the organisation adopts the approach described as Option A, those funding the service will be asked to top up the £2,000 by £100 to £2,100 (100 times £1). If Option B is adopted, with the budget based on expected price levels, an allowance will be built into the budget to cover anticipated future rises in price. If the person preparing the budget has perfect foresight they will estimate that the effect of future inflation will be 5% and the budget would be £2,100 (£2,000 plus 5%). As few people can forecast inflation perfectly, the approved budget will normally prove to be too low or high, depending on the estimated and actual rates of inflation. If, for example, at the point at which the budget was set the expected effect of inflation next year was 3%, the budget would have been as shown in Table 7.6.

If no managerial action is taken, the budget will be overspent by £40 by the year end. Alternatively, if the budget manager tries to keep within budget only 98 cartridges (98*£21=£2,058) will be purchased, resulting in an underspend of £2 (£2,060 less £2,058).

One common response to the current financial situation is for organisations to declare that there will be no top up in the event that inflation occurs. The implication of this is that the volume of spending will need to fall to keep within the approved budget; it is a form of budget cut that will increase in significance given recent forecast increases in inflation.

Table 7.6 The effect of inflation on budgets – example

Budget	£
At current prices (100 cartridges at £20)	2,000
Anticipated effect of inflation (3% on £2000)	60
Total budget	2,060
Actual expenditure (100 at £21)	2,100
Potential overspend	40

TIPS FOR SUCCESS

As a budget holder, make sure that you understand how inflation is treated in your organisation, the implications this has for your budget and how you may need to manage during the year.

- *If the prices prevailing when the budget was prepared (Option A) are used you should find out whether additional budget will be paid if prices rise.*
- *If future prices are used (Option B) you should find out the rate of inflation that was used and reach a view as to the adequacy of this provision. Be prepared to challenge the rate(s) of inflation used and monitor the prices actually incurred during the year.*

Employee budgets

For many managers in health and social care the largest budget relates to employee costs; in practice, this budget is often so large that, if not managed properly, it will inevitably have a significant affect on the overall budget position.

While incremental and zero-based approaches to budget preparation can be used with employee budgets, there are three other common approaches; full staff establishment, anticipated staff cost and mid scale.

Full staff establishment

With this approach the employee budget is based on the staff structure and terms and conditions of employment expected to apply during the budget year, together with the grade and spinal column points relating to current post holders. For each existing post holder an estimate is made of the salary they will receive next year including increments, performance related pay and annual pay awards, etc. If there are anticipated changes to the staffing structure or terms and conditions these will be incorporated, as will currently vacant posts at appropriate rates.

This approach should lead to a budget that will be sufficient to meet the cost of employing staff next year. In practice, this often leads to an underspend due to members of staff leaving and not being replaced for some time, and new staff being appointed low on the pay scale.

This approach should not be confused with zero-based budgeting as no attempt is made to challenge, for example, the current staff establishment, skill mix or remuneration packages.

Anticipated staff costs

When staff budgets are underspent due to staff turnover, this can prove embarrassing as the money saved could have been used for additional service provision. A common way of trying to avoid this problem is to deduct from the full staff establishment budget, as described above, an amount equal to the savings expected to arise from staff turnover.

There are, however, a number of drawbacks with this approach:

- the budget manager starts the year with a budget that will be insufficient to meet their staff costs should they experience zero staff turnover;
- estimating the impact of future staff turnover is difficult as it is affected by such factors as role, age, gender, seniority and economic environment;
- where staff budgets are devolved, the number of staff within a cost centre may be relatively few which means that the actual experience of turnover is likely to vary significantly from one cost centre to another and from one year to the next;
- in practice, some staff vacancies may have to be covered through overtime or the use of agency staff, the cost of which may well be greater than the savings released. For a few services there is a case to be made for adding a factor for turnover rather than deducting it.

Mid scale

Another approach to calculating employee budgets, which is attractive because it is simple and easy to use, is 'mid scale'. Irrespective of the spinal column points on which actual staff will be paid, the budget is based on the midpoint of the scale. The example below is of a cost centre employing ten full time staff on a grade that starts at £15,000 and rises in five equal increments to £19,000.

In a financial 'worst case' scenario, all staff would be on the top of the scale and expected expenditure would therefore be £190,000, whereas the budget is based on £170,000. In the event that there is no staff turnover the budget will be £20,000 overspent at the end of the year.

In practice, the budget is normally set too low to meet the cost of staff in post and an overspend will occur unless there is sufficient turnover to provide offsetting savings. Occasionally, however, the budget will be too generous, for example, where the service is new or there has been significant turnover in recent years with new staff recruited on low incremental points.

Issues for budget managers

Different ways of calculating employee budgets leave the manager with different potential gaps between the budget and the total amount they may need to pay their staff next year. As a

Table 7.7 Mid scale approach to employee budget – example

Scale point	Salary	Mid point	Number of staff	Budget
5	£19,000			
4	£18,000			
3	£17,000	£17,000	10	£170,000
2	£16,000			
1	£15,000			

budget manager, it is important to understand how the budget has been prepared, the assumptions made and the size of any potential gap between the budget and likely spending on staff.

Another potential issue for the manager is whether they have financial responsibility for any other employee-related costs that may or may not be allowed for in their agreed budget, for example, costs associated with long-term sickness and maternity. These can be difficult to predict, volatile over time and significant in size.

TIPS FOR SUCCESS

If you have responsibility for a staff budget you should:

- *Calculate how much you think your staff will cost next year, assuming no staff turnover.*
- *Identify the organisation's approach to estimating employee budgets and establish the resultant budget figure.*
- *Calculate the difference between (1) and (2) above, identifying whether a potential under-/overspend is likely.*
- *Consistent with good budget practice, alert your line manager to any potential under-/overspend as early as possible.*
- *Plan how to manage any under/overspend. In most cases there is likely to be a potential overspend which, without employee turnover, will be very difficult to meet. However, it is the responsibility of the budget manager to take reasonable steps to offset any overspends through action related to other expenditure or income budgets.*

In addition you should establish:

- *Whether budget responsibility for staffing includes meeting the financial consequences of long-term sickness or maternity cover and whether this is allowed for in your budget.*
- *Whether the budget includes a reasonable allowance for the expected effect of future pay awards.*
- *What will happen if the annual pay award is settled at a rate different to that assumed in the budget?*

Section 8
Budgetary control

This section explains the budgetary control process, introduces profiling and commitment recording, and explains how to read a budget report, undertake budgetary control and prepare a year end forecast.

Budgetary control

Budgetary control is the process by which managers check and respond to the evolving position of actual income and expenditure budgets during the year. At its simplest the process involves:

- checking that financial information is accurate;
- comparing actual income and expenditure figures with what was expected up to this point in the year and identifying and investigating any significant differences, or variances;
- projecting the likely budget position at the year end and taking action as required.

Budgetary control should not be a standalone process; rather, it should be an integral part of performance management. Effective budgetary control:

- causes budget managers to engage with, and act upon, financial information;
- permits the early identification of potential underspends in a way that enables action resulting in the best use of resources, rather than perhaps a year end 'spend up';
- permits the early identification of potential overspends, this allowing gentle corrective action rather than the more brutal action needed when overspending becomes apparent towards the year end. Early action reduces the likelihood that clients fail to receive the standard of service they need, avoids staff being put under intense and unnecessary pressure and helps preserve performance and morale;
- reduces the likelihood of 'stop/go' purchasing and the consequential negative impact on clients, staff and other stakeholders;
- is a source of organisational learning.

Reporting process

The process of reporting and acting on budget variance varies between organisations, ranging from those where budgetary control appears to be the responsibility of:

- Finance staff who in practice can only go so far before having to ask the budget manager for help to understand important variances, and take action. In this type of organisation it is common to find senior managers and politicians turning to accountants for budget information rather than their budget managers. There is an associated risk that the manager believes that the accountant is 'looking after the money' and, therefore, engages even less in the financial aspects of their role; a vicious circle is created.

- Managers who assume full budget responsibility and are assisted by finance staff who provide financial information and technical support, along with corporate level strategic budget monitoring. Budget estimation, negotiation, approval and control are all exercised within the managerial line.

Three key questions

There are three key questions that typically provide the focus for budgetary control:

- How are we doing?
- How much of the budget is left?
- What will the year end position look like?

While a few managers will consider all these questions, more will typically focus on only one or two of these, according to organisational practice and/or personal preference.

1. How are we doing?

This question focuses entirely on what has happened so far in the current budget year. Table 8.1 provides budget information for the first five months of the year in respect of stationery. The budget for the whole year is £12,000 and expenditure is expected to be even throughout the year.

At this point in the year the budget is underspent by £88.

In this example, an underspend is shown as negative whereas an overspend would be positive. With regard to how underspends and overspends are shown on budget reports there is little consistency between, and sometimes even within, organisations. Plusses, minuses, brackets and colours are all used and the manager should always check they understand the approach to presenting underspends and overspends prior to reading a financial report.

Table 8.1 shows the cumulative position, that is all expenditure up to and including that occurring in month five. In some organisations this will be accompanied by the same information but relating to the last month as shown in Table 8.2, which shows that £80 of the £88 underspending occurred in August.

2. How much of the budget is left?

Knowing how much budget is left to spend at a point in the year is important information, calculated by deducting actual expenditure to date from the budget for the whole year. Returning to the earlier example, it appears that £7,088 (£12,000-£4,912) is left to be spent.

Table 8.1 Budgetary control – example 1

Budget for £12,000	Budget to 31 August	Actual to 31 August	Variance to 31 August
	£	£	£
Stationery	5,000	4,912	–88

Table 8.2 Budgetary control – example 2

Budget for the year £12,000	Budget for August	Actual for August	Variance for August	Budget for year to 31 August	Actual for year to 31 August	Variance for year to 31 August
	£	£	£	£	£	£
Stationery	1,000	920	−80	5,000	4,912	−88

3. What will the year end position look like?

Ultimately, budget performance is judged on whether the manager keeps within the budget for the whole year. Overspends and underspends at various points in the year tend to be forgotten if, at the year end, spending is within budget and income is equal to, or in excess of, that budgeted.

Increasingly, the practice within organisations is to make regular estimates of the final year end position. These figures are known variously as estimated outturn, projected outturn, forecast year end and budget holder forecast.

In practice, there are two main ways of estimating the year end, either by:

- Reference to actual income and expenditure at the current point in the year. So, if stationery expenditure at month five is £4,912, the year end prediction figure would be £11,788, arrived at by dividing the actual to date by the number of months it relates to and multiplying by 12.

$$\frac{\text{Actual to date}}{\text{Months to date}} \times 12 \quad \frac{£4,912}{5} \times 12 = £11,788$$

For those budgets where broadly the same amount of money will be spent each month, this approach is fine. However, for many budgets the rate of spend varies during the year and predictions calculated this way can be seriously flawed. Returning to the stationery example, for which there is a total budget for the year of £12,000 – if, instead of spending approximately the same amount each month, the practice is to bulk purchase £5,000 of stationery by the end of April, the predicted outturn at month one using this basis would be £60,000 (£5,000/1*12)!

or

- Combining the actual to date with an estimate of expenditure or income for the rest of the year. As this calculation is best done by the budget manager this should really be referred to as a budget manager forecast. This figure should take account of spend to date, reasons for any variance to date plus anticipated spend for the rest of the year.

Profiling

One key piece of information needed for budgetary control purposes is the amount of the budget that it is expected to be spent or earned by a particular point in time, often referred to as the 'budget to date', or budget profile in budgetary control statements.

In effect, the annual budget comprises twelve monthly budgets, the relative size of each being determined by factors such as service activity, weather and contracts of employment.

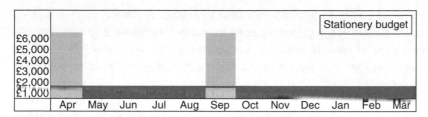

Figure 8.1 Profile and actual comparison (based on an incorrect 'even' profile)

Good quality profiling is essential to good budgetary control; however, it is still quite common to find budget statements where the profile is simply assumed to be 'even' each month. This practice can be very misleading, as shown in Figure 8.1, which concerns a stationery budget where the practice is to bulk buy in April and September, each time spending 50 per cent of the budget. Actual spending is shown in grey and the 'even' budget profile in black.

Based on these figures a budgetary control statement would incorrectly show an overspend for most of the year – at the end of April the overspend would be £5,000 (£1,000 profiled budget less £6,000 of actual spending). This overspend would reduce each month to September when it would increase to £6,000 (£12,000 of total spending less £6,000 of profiled budget). From October onwards the overspend would decrease each month and, assuming that no more expenditure occurs during the year, the total spending at the year end would be identical to the original budget. All the overspend figures for the first eleven months are incorrect due to inappropriate profiling and could cause the reader to misunderstand the budget position and take inappropriate control action.

TIPS FOR SUCCESS

- *A good budget manager knows the budget needed to deliver the plan and the pattern of expected spend over the year.*

Commitments

Main accounting systems vary in terms of the point at which a transaction is recorded and becomes formally 'known' in the organisation.

In many public sector organisations, income appears on the main accounting system at the earliest opportunity with cash, cheques, etc., appearing when they are banked and invoice income as soon as invoices are issued. Income figures, therefore, tend to be reasonably up to date, something which is not always true of expenditure figures. Traditionally, many local authority accounting systems recognise expenditure only when payments are made rather than when orders were issued. As a consequence, expenditure will be understated where services have been received but invoices have yet to be paid.

As it is important to have up-to-date income and expenditure information during the year, it is common practice to combine payment information from the main system with local information regarding outstanding orders, etc., when undertaking budgetary control.

Commitment recording systems record information in respect of orders raised, deliveries received and invoices passed for payment. At present, many commitment systems are still manual or involve the use of spreadsheets. The need for these local systems will decline with new accounting systems that incorporate online order processing and hold commitment information. If it is necessary to design new local commitment systems it is wise to ask finance staff for advice regarding the format. Of crucial importance is ensuring that budget to date information (profile) and commitment information are on a comparable basis and that those using this understand any assumptions made.

EXAMPLE

This example relates to a budget of £100,000 of which £80,000 is expected (profiled) to have been spent by the end of month eight.

Payments of £73,500 appear on the computer and at first glance it appears that this budget is underspent by £6,500 (£80,000 – £73,500) and £26,500 (£100,000 – £73,500) remains in the budget. However, assuming in this example that the total value of official orders issued but not yet paid is £7,500, the position is actually quite different as shown in Table 8.3. In order to get a more realistic view of actual spending and what is left the value of outstanding orders needs to be taken into account.

Table 8.3 Commitment recording – example

Budget for year		£100,000
	£	£
Profiled budget (months 1–8)		80,000
Payments (months 1–8)	73,500	
Commitments (months 1–8)	7,500	
Expenditure (months 1–8)		81,000
Budget position (overspent at month 8)		1,000
Budget remaining		19,000

When operating a commitment system it is essential to ensure regular reconciliation with the actual expenditure recorded on the main accounting system.

Understanding budget reports

While budget report formats vary from one organisation to the next, and even within an organisation, the extent of variation tends to be fairly limited and tends to concern the order in which information is provided and terminology used, both of which reflect the traditions of the organisation and preferences of finance staff. Figure 8.2 is an extract from a typical budget report, together with an explanation as to the content.

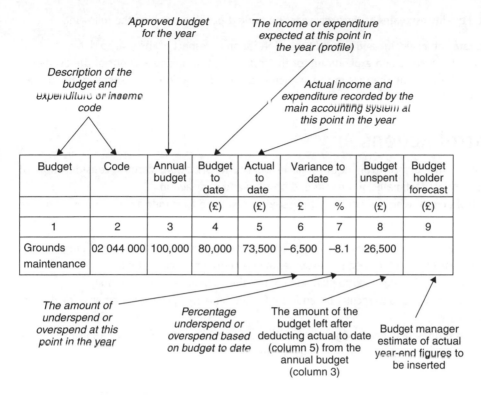

Figure 8.2 Example budget report

When reading a budget statement the budget manager should ensure they understand:

- how the Annual Budget (column 3) was prepared, the plan it links to and whether it includes an allowance for inflation;
- how the budget has been profiled (column 4) and be assured that this is realistic;
- how up to date the actual figure (column 5) is and be prepared to add to this any expenditure that is committed but has not yet been taken into account;
- how underspends and overspends are shown on the system and be clear as to what constitutes a significant variance (columns 6 and 7);
- the accuracy of the budget unspent figure and how this will need to change if any commitments have to be taken into account;
- what is expected of them regarding the budget manager forecast and be able to prepare appropriate figures.

Forecasting the year end

Of increasing importance to understanding the budget position is the ability of the budget manager to estimate year end figures.

Where organisations devolve budget responsibility, effective control is dependent on managers more than accountants and there is an opportunity to move away from pro rata year end of year calculations and adopt budget manager estimates.

Good quality estimates of the likely year end budget position combine the following:

- accurate actual income and expenditure information in respect of the year to date;
- anticipated income and expenditure for the rest of the year taking account of the estimated financial impact of changes in the service and intended actions in respect of any under-spend and overspend to date.

Control actions

Effective budgetary control requires good quality information, careful consideration of variances, honest estimates of the year end position and early action.

Control action, which is normally triggered in response to significant variances, can take many forms, including for example:

1. Taking steps to increase or decrease service volume and quality over the remaining months of the year to bring the need for resources in line with remaining budget.
2. Reminding staff of the need to plan and control their use of resources carefully.
3. Delaying committing particular expenditure for the time being or even, perhaps, for the rest of the year.
4. Moving money between budgets; a practice common in some voluntary and most public sector organisations, and referred to as 'virement'.

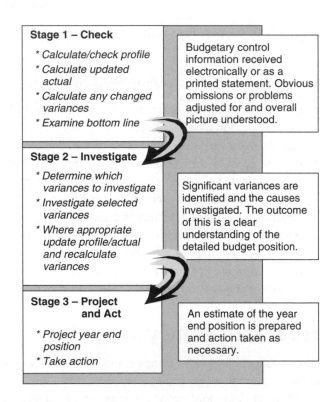

Figure 8.3 Budgetary control stages

Undertaking budgetary control

When undertaking budgetary control, care should be taken to avoid two risks: spending excessive time on the process and missing potentially significant variances. Small underspends or overspends are inevitable for almost every budget and the effective budget manager will focus on those variances that, without action, might develop into something significant. This ability to spot potential problems requires knowledge of the service plan, experience of service operation and, ultimately, sound judgement.

Budgetary control should be undertaken on a monthly basis by the manager responsible and supported by administrative staff and accountants. The process can be seen as comprising three stages, all of which are important and are the responsibility of the budget manager, although not necessarily undertaken by them personally. Figure 8.3 illustrates these three stages. Depending on the systems and processes that are in place, Stage 1 could be undertaken by administrative staff, particularly if they also are responsible for maintaining commitment records. With appropriate guidance regarding how to identify significant variances, these staff might also undertake Stage 2.

Stage 3, however, should always be completed personally by the responsible budget manager as only they will have the appropriate knowledge and skills needed to complete the year end forecast and the authority to take management action. The following example explains this process in detail.

EXAMPLE

This example relates to a day centre for older people. The budget manager is responsible for four budgets and is required to keep actual expenditure within budget for each.

The annual budget includes an allowance for the effect of future inflation and the budget to date is based on the amount that it is expected will be spent by this point in the year. Copier payments are monthly by direct debit. There is £500 of food which has been ordered, used and in respect of which the invoice has been passed for payment – however, this is not included in the actual to date. The printout covers the first six months of the financial year, April to September.

Table 8.4 Budgetary control – example 3

Budget	Annual budget	Budget to date	Actual to date	Variance to date		Budget unspent	Budget forecast
		(£)	(£)	£	%	(£)	(£)
Copier rental	1,200	600	600	0	0	600	
Copier usage	600	250	299	49	20	301	
Gas	2,400	960	734	−226	24	1,666	
Food	10,000	4,200	3,951	−249	6	6,049	
Total	14,200	6,010	5,584	−426	7	8,616	

Taking this example and following through the three main stages outlined in Figure 8.3:

Stage 1 – Check

The first thing to note is that the overall budget expected to have been spent at this point in the year is £6,010 while actual expenditure is lower at £5,584 – an underspend at this point of £426 which, on the face of it, appears good news. There are, perhaps, no obvious problems with the profile behind the budget to date figures. A check of transactions reveals that the actual food expenditure is lower than it should be by £500 due to a commitment. If the invoice is included, actual food expenditure would be £4,451 resulting in an overspend of £251 for food and changing the overall surplus of £426 into a deficit of £74.

Stage 2 – Investigate

When deciding which variances to investigate a number of factors come into play, including:

1. Size of variance (expressed in £s) – for many managers, this is the most important criterion, causing attention to be focused on large amounts of money. There is no golden rule as to what constitutes a large variance as this depends on a number of factors, particularly context.
2. Size of variance (expressed as a percentage) – percentages are a popular criterion, often associated with a threshold figure above which an investigation is triggered, e.g. 5 per cent. This approach poses one significant risk in that a large percentage variance on a small budget might trigger interest while a small percentage variance on a larger budget could go unnoticed, even though it might be of a much higher monetary value.
3. Knowledge of the service – a good budget manager who has been actively engaged in budget preparation will have a sense of which budgets are more volatile or sensitive and, therefore, need to be watched carefully.

It should be noted that underspends and overspends are of equal concern. Looking at each budget in turn for the purpose of this exercise.

Copier rental is on track – the budget to date is based on a regular amount each month, which has been paid. There is no under/overspend and the amount left for the rest of the year looks adequate.

Copier usage – currently overspent by £49 (20%); there could be some problems at the year end if this continues. The sum involved is not great but it might be worth raising this at the next team meeting and monitoring this next control period.

Gas – underspent by £226 (24%). This variance is quite large and raises questions as to the validity of the profile and whether the expected number of quarterly bills has been paid. If one bill is outstanding then the 'real actual' will be quite a bit higher possibly making this overspent rather than underspent.

Food – underspent by £249 (6%) but after adjusting for the commitment is actually overspent by £251 (6%). This is not a large overspend in terms of the amount or percentage involved but might need to be watched as this is a budget where control can be lost quite quickly. It would be worth mentioning this to the chef and looking at it again next month.

Of the four budgets it can be argued that only gas needs investigating while copier usage and food would be worth mentioning to staff and then monitoring.

The process of investigation involves looking at the detailed transactions that make up the recorded expenditure to check that these relate to the service involved, are complete and correct. A comparison can then be made with the budget profile in terms of what was expected, for example, were two gas bills included in the profile but only one has been paid. If the correct number of bills has been paid, investigating the underspend might reveal a number of causes, for example, that:

1. The price paid for gas is lower than was expected when the budget was set.
2. Less gas has been consumed than expected.

Stage 3 – Project and act

At this point, the budget manager should understand the overall budget position, be aware of any significant underspends or overspends and the causes.

Two further steps need to be completed – estimating the year end and taking action.

Estimating the likely year end budget position involves taking account of experience so far this year and estimating future service resource needs. Table 8.5 is one possible format for undertaking a budget holder forecast.

Information for the first three columns is as shown in the latest budget report. Column 3 might need to be adjusted depending on the outcome of any variance investigations, for example, if a gas bill had been coded elsewhere in the organisation. Column 4 is an estimate of the expenditure that will be needed for the rest of the year, reflecting a number of factors, including anything learnt as a result of the investigation. Column 5 is the budget manager forecast, simply the sum of columns 3 and 4. Column 6 shows the variance for the year calculated as the difference between columns 2 and 5.

Table 8.5 Budget manager forecast 1

Budget	Annual budget	Actual months 1–6	Estimate months 7–12	Budget manager forecast	Variance for year
1	2	3	4	5	6
	£	£	£	£	£
Gas	2,400	734	?	?	?

EXAMPLE

Assuming the investigation reveals that:

- *two gas bills have been paid as expected, are correctly coded and error free;*
- *gas consumption is at the level expected;*
- *the underspend is entirely due to a 24% reduction in gas prices that is predicted to continue for the foreseeable future.*

The figure to be included in column 4 can be calculated in different ways, for example, starting with the budget that was originally expected to be needed for the last six months of the year (£2,400 for the year less £960 for the first six months) which equals £1,440. As gas prices have fallen by 24% below what was expected, one view of the rest of the year is that it will cost £1,094 (£1,440 less 24%).

Column 5 is simply the result of adding £734 plus £1,094 which equals £1,828. Column 6 is the variance for the whole year, this resulting from a comparison of the budget with the budget manager forecast.

Table 8.6 Budget manager forecast 2

Budget	Annual budget	Actual months 1–6	Estimate months 7–12	Budget manager forecast	Variance for year
1	2	3	4	5	6
	£	£	£	£	£
Gas	2,400	734	1,094	1,828	–572

With regard to this budget there is a reasonable predicted underspend. The manager may wish to leave this sum where it is for the moment or vire (transfer) part or all of it to another budget where it can be used to fund an overspending situation or even boost spending in an area where there is an identified service need.

This is, of course, only one view of the future based on an assumption that prices remain lower than budgeted. A different and more prudent view would be that prices return to budgeted levels for the rest of the year in which case the budget manager forecast would be £2,174 (£734 actual to date plus £1,440 which was the original budget for the rest of the year).

A final note here is that a good budget manager will consider their budgets individually and on a collective basis. The answer to a problem on one budget, for example, copier usage, may be to control another one, for example gas, more closely.

Section 9
Managing budgets in an economic downturn

For most public sector organisations, spending has been under pressure for many years. Demand for services, rising aspirations and attempts to limit resources have combined to apply pressure on budgets. Periodically, central government attempts to reduce spending through initiatives such as value for money, best value and efficiency drives. Often, the outcome of these initiatives is an incremental reduction in spending or what is often referred to as 'salami slicing'.

The current economic downturn prompted significant budget reductions in spending in 2011/12 which look set to be repeated for several more years. The scale and speed of these cuts pose a significant challenge to leaders that cannot be met by incremental reduction alone. Innovation and a departure from conventional approaches to planning, budgeting and operating is required; the public service paradigm needs to shift.

Economy, efficiency and effectiveness

Budget reductions generally result from a decision to cease or reduce the quantity or quality of service or improvements in economy, efficiency or operational effectiveness. Figure 9.1 shows how economy, efficiency and effectives combine to result in value for money

Economy improvements include better procurement and reduced staff costs.

Efficiency improvements include collaborating to share services, integrating delivery pathways and eliminating waste.

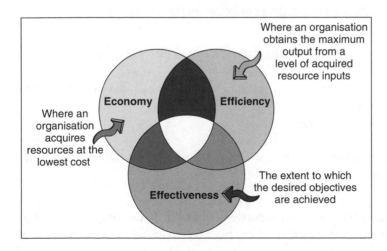

Figure 9.1 *Value for money components*

Effectiveness improvements include reviewing service user needs so that services can be focused on what is important.

Drives to reduce expenditure often appear to impact in ways that have not been anticipated, causing, for example, costs to fall on other budgets, other parts of an organisation, other agencies, current service users or the next generation of citizens.

A decision, for example, to buy cheaper paper for a photocopier will result in lower stationery spending but if this results in more paper jams then staff efficiency will fall. A reduction in building maintenance will result in lower spending for a while but future taxpayers will eventually have to meet the cost. A decision to spend less on care for the elderly results in greater demands on families and potentially an increased call on paramedic services. When implementing cuts quickly, particularly significant ones, care should therefore be taken to look at the impact:

- across economy, efficiency and effectiveness as it is easy for improvements in one to be offset elsewhere;
- in the long term as well as short term;
- on other agencies, service users and carers or, more generally, society.

Three responses

Currently, the responses of public service leaders to an unprecedented need for budget reduction can be grouped in three ways.

1. Incremental reductions in net spending including:
   - percentage non-pay budget reductions;
   - frozen pay;
   - removal of managerial tiers;
   - downgrading work activities causing more junior staff to take on responsibilities previously undertaken by their manager;
   - increases in fees, charges and taxes.

While incremental approaches may reduce net spending, the yield tends to be relatively small, short term and causes indiscriminate damage to outcomes. Furthermore, the lack of transparency associated with many of these approaches tends to perpetuate the illusion that it is possible to cut net spending without affecting services or users.

2. Step reductions in planned net spending such as:
   - elimination or scaling back of non-statutory services or non-essential spending;
   - pay rate reductions;
   - service reviews targeted at significant spending reductions by reducing the quantity and/or quality of services;
   - intra-organisation process redesign;
   - sharing of services and mergers;
   - selling of in-house services to existing or new markets, e.g., payroll to other public service organisations;
   - selling assets.

These approaches can offer significant reductions in planned spending as a result of reduced service volume, better user targeting, quality reduction or adopting different means of service delivery. While the transparency and honesty associated with these approaches is welcome, the potential impact on users and the community may be adverse and significant.

3. Other measures

There is a third set of measures which impact on the level of spending and these include:

- temporary non-filling of vacant posts;
- cessation of spending on certain purchases, for example, refreshments, external venues for training and meetings;
- more senior staff making spending decisions – e.g. the use of care panels;
- declared maximum rates to be paid to consultants, for beds in residential homes, etc.;
- inviting suppliers to reduce prices in response to market conditions.

The next five years will see reduced scope for incremental budget reductions as inefficiency within the existing paradigm is progressively eliminated. The scope for, and yield from, step reductions will also fall unless there are changes in legislation regarding statutory services.

The scale and manner of current budget reduction is the equivalent of organisational crash dieting and three classic problems need to be avoided:

- organisations that fall below a viable weight – in order to meet statutory responsibilities and meet electoral pledges, each local authority has, in effect, a minimum viable weight. Reducing spending to below this level will incur potentially serious consequences;
- losing weight in the wrong places – budget reductions can result in a situation where some services are largely unaffected whilst others become unviable;
- post-diet weight gain – many approaches to organisational dieting fail to keep the pounds off as:
  - stakeholders make compelling cases for controlled weight gain in areas where the impact of a crash diet is deemed unacceptable;
  - over time, informal local adjustments are made to systems to cope with the impact of cuts;
  - system upgrades are introduced to cope with new legislation and changes in demand and service;
  - bad habits develop and go unchecked.

Over time, the impact of the above will cause increased spending and a drift towards inefficiency.

TIPS FOR SUCCESS

When dealing with financial constraint and budget reduction it is wise to:

- *consider both the long and short term;*
- *consider the impact on other organisations and the wider community;*
- *be clear about the level of savings sought;*
- *take into account inflation;*
- *maintain the link between plan and budget;*
- *think about the potential impact of cuts on behaviour;*
- *understand whether savings are due to economy, efficiency or effectiveness and look for unintended outcomes.*

Conclusion

The intention behind writing this text was to promote effective planning and budget management and prompt the development of associated competence. The content provides a starting point for achieving this aim and, with practice, you should feel able to use the techniques included with competence and confidence. There is, however, considerable scope for further personal development by extending your repertoire of planning techniques and knowledge of cost behaviour and analysis. The books referred to in the References section are a good initial source of learning for anyone wishing to further develop their competence in planning and budget management.

References

Bean, J. and Hussey, L. (1996) *Managing the Devolved Budget*. London: HB Publications.

CIPFA (2001) *Financial Regulations: A Good Practice Guide for an English Modern Council*. London: CIPFA Publications.

Drury, C. (1994) *Costing: An Introduction* (3rd edition). London: Chapman Hall.

Johnson, G., Scholes, K. and Whittington, R. (2008) *Exploring Corporate Strategy* (8th edition). Harlow: Pearson Education.

Luffman, G., Sanderson, S. and Kenny, B. (1987) *Business Policy: An Analytical Introduction*. Massachusetts: Blackwell.

Mintzberg, H. (1994) The fall and rise of strategy planning. *Harvard Business Review*, Jan–Feb: 106–14.

Mintzberg, H., Ahlstrand, B. and Lampel, J. (1998) *Strategy Safari*. Harlow: Prentice Hall.

Moore, M. (1995) *Creating Public Value Strategic Management in Government*. Cambridge, MA: Harvard University Press.

Semple Piggot, C. (2000) *Business Planning for Healthcare Management*. Milton Keynes: Open University Press.

Index